The Development of Political Institutions

Herbert Spencer

The Development of Political Institutions

LM Publishers

I. Preliminary

Thought and feeling cannot be completely dissociated. Each emotion has a more or less distinct framework of ideas; and each group of ideas is more or less suffused with emotion. There are, however, great differences between their degrees of combination under both of these aspects. We have some feelings which are vague from lack of intellectual definition; and others to which clear shapes are given by the associated conceptions. At one time our thoughts are distorted by the passion running through them; and at another time it is difficult to detect in them a trace of liking or . disliking. Manifestly, too, in each particular case these components of the mental state may be varied in their proportions. The ideas being the same, the emotion joined with them may be greater or less; and it is a familiar truth that the correctness of the judgment formed depends, if not on the absence of emotion, still, on that balance of emotions which negatives excess of any one.

Especially is this so in matters concerning human life. There are two ways in which men's actions, individual or social, may be regarded. We may consider them as groups of phenomena to be analyzed, and the laws of their dependence ascertained; or, considering them as causing pleasures or pains, we may associate with them approbation or reprobation. Dealing with its problems intellectually, we may regard conduct as always the result of certain forces; or dealing with its problems morally, and considering its outcome as in this case good and in that case bad, we may allow now admiration, and now indignation, to fill our consciousness. Obviously, it must make a great difference in our conclusions whether, as in the one case, we regard men's doings as those of alien creatures, which it merely concerns us to understand; or whether, as in the other case, we regard them as the doings of creatures like ourselves, with whose lives our own lives are bound up, and whose behavior arouses in us, directly and sympathetically, feelings of love and hate.

In "The Study of Sociology," I have described in detail the various perversions produced in men's judgments by their emotions. Examples are given showing how fears and hopes betray them into false estimates; how impatience prompts unjust condemnations; how in this case antipathy, and in that case sympathy, distorts belief. The truth that the bias of education and the bias of patriotism severally warp men's convictions, is enforced by many illustrations. And it is pointed out that the more special forms of bias—the class bias, the political bias, the theological bias—each produces a strong predisposition toward this or that view of public affairs.

Here let me emphasize the conclusion that in pursuing our sociological inquiries, and especially those on which we are now entering, we must, as much as possible, exclude whatever emotions the facts are calculated to excite, and attend solely to the interpretation of the facts. There are several groups of phenomena, in contemplating which either contempt, or disgust, or indignation, tends to arise, but must be restrained.

Instead of passing over as of no account, or else regarding as purely mischievous, the superstitions of the primitive man, we must inquire what part they play in social evolution; and must be prepared, if need be, to recognize their usefulness. Already we have seen that the belief which prompts the savage to bury valuables with the corpse and carry food to the grave has a natural genesis; that the propitiation of plants and animals and the "worship of stocks and stones" are not gratuitous absurdities; and that slaves are sacrificed at funerals in pursuance of an idea which seems rational to uninstructed intelligence. Presently we shall have to consider in what way the ghost-theory has operated politically; and, if we should find reason to conclude that it has been an indispensable aid to social evolution, we must be ready to accept the conclusion.

Knowledge of the miseries that have for countless ages been everywhere caused by the antagonisms of societies must not prevent us from recognizing the all-important part which these antagonisms have played in civilization. Shudder as we must at the cannibalism which all over the world in early days was a sequence of war; shrink as we may from the thought of those immolations of prisoners which have, tens of thousands of times, followed battles between wild tribes; read as we do with horror of the pyramids of heads and the whitening bones of slain peoples left by barbarian invaders; hate, as we ought, the militant spirit which is even now among ourselves prompting base treacheries and brutal aggressions—we must not let our feelings blind us to the proofs we meet with, that intersocial conflicts have furthered the development of social structures.

Moreover, dislikes to governments of certain kinds must not prevent us from seeing their fitnesses to their circumstances. Though rejecting the common idea of glory, and declining to join soldiers and schoolboys in applying the epithet "great" to conquering despots, we detest despotism; though we regard their sacrifices of their own peoples and of alien peoples in pursuit of universal dominion as gigantic crimes—we must yet recognize the benefits occasionally arising from the social consolidations they achieve. Neither the massacres of subjects which Roman emperors directed, nor the assassinations of relatives habitual among potentates in the East, nor the impoverishment of whole nations by the excessive exactions of tyrants, must so prejudice us as to prevent appreciation of the benefits which have, under certain conditions, resulted from the unlimited power of the supreme man. Nor must the remembrances of torturing implements, and *oubliettes,* and victims built into walls, shut out from our minds the evidence that abject submission of the weak to the strong, however unscrupulously enforced, has in some times and places been necessary.

So, too, with the associated ownership of man by man. Absolute condemnation of slavery must be withheld, even if we accept the tradition repeated by Herodotus, that to build the Great Pyramid relays of a hundred thousand slaves toiled for twenty years; or even if we find it true that, of the serfs compelled to work at the building of St. Petersburg, three hundred thousand perished. Though aware that the unrecorded sufferings of men and women held in bondage are beyond imagination, we must, nevertheless, preserve a mental state receptive of such evidence as there may be that benefits have resulted.

In brief, trustworthy interpretations of social arrangements imply an almost passionless consciousness. Though feeling cannot and ought not to be excluded from the mind when otherwise contemplating them, yet it ought to be excluded when contemplating them as natural phenomena to be understood in their causes and effects.

Maintenance of this mental attitude will be furthered by keeping before ourselves the truth that in human actions the absolutely bad may be relatively good, and the absolutely good may be relatively bad.

Though it has become a commonplace that the institutions under which one race prospers will not answer for another, the recognition of this truth is by no means adequate. Men who have lost faith in "paper constitutions," nevertheless advocate a policy toward inferior races, implying the belief that civilized social forms can with advantage be imposed on uncivilized peoples; that the arrangements which seem to us vicious are vicious for them; and that they would benefit by institutions— domestic, industrial, or political—akin to those which we find beneficial. But acceptance of the truth that the type of a society is determined by the natures of its units, forces on us the corollary that a *régime* intrinsically of the lowest may yet be the best possible under primitive conditions.

Otherwise stating the matter, we must not substitute our developed code of conduct, which predominantly concerns private relations, for the undeveloped code of conduct which predominantly concerns public relations. Now that life is generally occupied in peaceful intercourse with fellow-citizens, ethical ideas refer chiefly to actions between man and man; but, in early stages, while the occupation of life was mainly in conflicts with adjacent societies, such ethical ideas as existed referred almost wholly to intersocial actions: men's deeds were judged by their direct bearings on tribal welfare. And since preservation of the society takes precedence of individual preservation, as being a condition to it, we must, in considering social phenomena, interpret good and bad rather in their earlier senses than in their later senses; and so must regard as relatively good that which furthers survival of the society, great as may be the suffering inflicted on individuals.

Another of our ordinary conceptions has to be much widened before we can rightly interpret political evolution. The words "civilized" and "savage" must have given to them meanings differing greatly from those which are current. That broad contrast usually drawn wholly to the advantage of the men who form advanced nations, and to the disadvantage of the men who form single groups, a better knowledge obliges us profoundly to qualify. Characters are to be found among rude peoples which compare well with those of the best among cultivated peoples. With little knowledge, and but rudimentary arts, there in some cases go virtues which might shame those among ourselves whose education and polish are of the highest.

Surviving remnants of some primitive races in India have natures in which truthfulness seems to be organic. Not only to the surrounding Hindoos, higher intellectually and relatively advanced in culture, are they in this respect far superior, but they are superior to Europeans. Of certain of these Hill peoples it is remarked in India that their assertions may always be accepted with perfect confidence; which is more than can be said of diplomatists who intentionally delude, or ministers who make false statements concerning cabinet transactions. As having this trait may be named the Santals, of whom Hunter says, "They were the most truthful set of men I ever met"; and, again, the Sowrahs, of whom Shortt says: "A pleasing feature in their character is their complete truthfulness. They do not know how to tell a lie." Notwithstanding their sexual relations

11

of a primitive and low type, even the Todas are described as considering "falsehood one of the worst of vices." Though Metz says that they practice dissimulation toward Europeans, yet he recognizes this as a trait consequent upon their intercourse with Europeans; and this judgment coincides with one given to me by an Indian civil servant concerning other Hill tribes, originally distinguished for their veracity, but who are rendered less veracious by contact with the whites. So rare is lying among these aboriginal races when unvitiated by the "civilized," that, of those in Bengal, Hunter singles out the Tipperahs as "the only Hill tribe in which this vice is met with."

Similarly in respect of honesty, some of those peoples classed as inferior read lessons to those classed as superior. Of the Todas just named, ignorant and degraded as they are in some respects, Harkness says, "I never saw a people, civilized or uncivilized, who seemed to have a more religious respect for the rights of *meum* and *tuum*." The Marias (Gonds), "in common with many other wild races, bear a singular character for truthfulness and honesty." Among the Khonds "the denial of a debt is a breach of this principle, which is held to be highly sinful. 'Let a man,' say they, 'give up all he has to his creditors.'" The Santal, who "never thinks of making money by a stranger," prefers to have "no dealings with his guests; but when his guests introduce the subject he deals with them as honestly as he would with his own people. . . he names the true price at first." The Lepchas "are wonderfully honest, theft being scarcely known among them." And the Bodo and Dhimáls are "honest and truthful in deed and word." Colonel Dixon dilates on the "fidelity, truth, and honesty" of the Carnatic aborigines; and they show "an extreme and almost touching devotion when put upon their honor." And Hunter asserts of the Chakmás, that "crime is rare among these primitive people. . . . Theft is almost unknown."

So it is, too, with the general virtues of these and sundry other uncivilized tribes. The Santal "possesses a happy disposition," is "sociable to a fault," "courteous," but "at the same time firm and free from cringing"; and, while the "sexes are greatly devoted to each other's society," the women are "exceedingly chaste." The Bodo and Dhimáls are "full of amiable qualities, and almost entirely free from such as are unamiable." The Lepcha, "cheerful, kind, and patient," is described by Dr. Hooker as a most "attractive companion"; and Dr. Campbell gives "an instance of the effect of a very strong sense of duty on this savage." In like manner, from accounts of certain of the Malayo-Polynesian societies, and certain of the Papuan societies, may be given instances showing in high degrees sundry traits which we ordinarily associate only with a human nature that has been long subject to the discipline of civilized life and the teachings of a superior religion. One of the latest testimonies is that of Signor D'Albertis, who describes certain New Guinea people he visited (near Yule Island) as strictly honest, "very kind," "good and peaceful," and who, after disputes between villages, "are as friendly as before, bearing no animosity"; but of whom the Rev. W. G. Lawes, commenting on Signor D'Albertis's communication to the Colonial Institute, says that their good-will to the whites is being destroyed by the whites' ill-treatment of them: the usual history.

Contrariwise, in various parts of the world, men of several types yield proofs that societies relatively advanced in organization and culture may yet be barbarous in their ideas, sentiments, and usages. The Feejeeans, described by Dr. Pickering as among the most intelligent of unlettered peoples, are among the most ferocious. "Intense and vengeful malignity strongly marks the Feejeean character." Lying, treachery, theft, and murder are with them not criminal, but honorable; infanticide is immense in extent; strangling the sickly habitual; and they sometimes cut up while alive the human victims they are going to eat. Nevertheless they have a "complicated and carefully conducted political system"; well-organized military forces; elaborate fortifications; a developed agriculture with succession of crops and irrigation; a considerable division of labor; a separate distributing agency with incipient currency;

13

and a skilled industry which builds canoes that carry three hundred men. Take again an African society, Dahomey. We find there a finished system of classes, six in number; complex governmental arrangements with officials always in pairs; an army divided into battalions, having reviews and sham-fights; prisons, police, and sumptuary laws; an agriculture which uses manure and grows a score kinds of plants; moated towns, bridges, and roads with turnpikes. Yet along with this comparatively high social development there goes what we may call organized criminality. Wars are made to get skulls with which to decorate the royal palace; hundreds of subjects are killed when the king dies; and five hundred are annually slaughtered to carry messages to the other world. Described as cruel and bloodthirsty, liars and cheats, the people are "void either of sympathy or gratitude, even in their own families," so that "not even the appearance of affection exists between husband and wife, or between parents and children." The New World, too, furnished, when it was discovered, like evidence. Having great cities of one hundred and eighty thousand houses, the Mexicans had also cannibal gods, whose idols were fed on warm, reeking, human flesh, thrust into their mouths— wars being made purposely to supply victims for them; and with skill to build stately temples, big enough for ten thousand men to dance in their courts, there went the immolation of twenty-five hundred persons annually, in Mexico and adjacent towns alone, and of a far greater number throughout the country at large. Similarly, in the populous Central American states, sufficiently civilized to have a developed system of calculation, a regular calendar, books, maps, etc., there were like extensive sacrifices of prisoners, slaves, children, whose hearts were torn out and offered palpitating on altars, and who, in other cases, were flayed alive and their skins used as dancing dresses by the priests.

Nor need we seek in remote regions or among alien races for proofs that there does not exist a necessary connection between the social types classed as civilized and those higher sentiments which we commonly associate with civilization.

The mutilations of prisoners exhibited on Assyrian sculptures are not surpassed in cruelty by any we find among the most bloodthirsty of wild races; and Rameses II, who delighted in having himself sculptured on temple-walls throughout Egypt as holding a dozen captives by the hair, and striking off their heads at a blow, slaughtered during his conquests more human beings than a thousand chiefs of savage tribes put together. The tortures inflicted on captured enemies by red Indians are not greater than were those inflicted of old on felons by crucifixion, or on suspected rebels by sewing them up in the hides of slaughtered animals, or on heretics by smearing them over with combustibles and setting fire to them. The Damaras, described as so utterly heartless that they laugh on seeing one of their number killed by a wild beast, are not worse than were the Romans, who made such elaborate provisions for gratifying themselves by watching wholesale slaughters in their arenas. If the numbers destroyed by the hordes of Attila were not equaled by the numbers which the Roman armies destroyed at the conquest of Selucia, and by the numbers of the Jews massacred under Hadrian, it was simply because the occasions did not permit. The cruelties of Nero, Gallienus, and the rest may compare with those of Genghis and Timour; and, when we read of Caracalla that, after he had murdered twenty thousand friends of his murdered brother, his soldiers forced the Senate to place him among the gods, we are shown that in the Roman people there was a ferocity not less than that which deifies the most sanguinary chiefs among the worst of savages. Nor. did Christianity greatly change matters. Throughout mediæval Europe political offenses and religious dissent brought on men carefully devised agonies equaling if not exceeding any inflicted by the most brutal of barbarians.

Startling as the truth seems, it is yet a truth to be recognized, that increase of humanity does not go on *pari passu* with civilization; but that, contrariwise, the earlier stages of civilization necessitate a relative inhumanity. Among tribes of primitive men, it is the more brutal rather than the more kindly who succeed in those conquests which effect the earliest social consolidations; and, through many subsequent stages of social evolution, unscrupulous aggression outside of the society and cruel coercion within are the habitual concomitants of political development. The men of whom the better organized societies have been formed were at first, and long continued to be, nothing else but the stronger and more cunning savages; and even now, when freed from those influences which superficially modify their behavior, they prove themselves to be little better. If, on the one hand, we contemplate the utterly uncivilized Wood-Veddahs, who are described as "proverbially truthful and honest," "gentle and affectionate," "obeying the slightest intimation of a wish, and very grateful for attention or assistance," and of whom Pridham remarks, "What a lesson in gratitude and delicacy even a Veddah may teach!" and then if, on the other hand, we contemplate our own recent acts of international brigandage, accompanied by the slaughter of thousands who have committed no wrong against us—accompanied, too, by perfidious breaches of faith and by the killing of prisoners in cold blood—we cannot but admit that, between the types of men classed as uncivilized and civilized, the differences are not necessarily of the kind commonly supposed. Whatever relation exists between moral nature and social type is not such as to imply that the social man is in all respects emotionally superior to the pre-social man.

"How is this conclusion to be reconciled with the conception of progress?" most readers will ask. "How is civilization to be justified if, as is thus implied, some of the highest of human attributes are exhibited in greater degrees by wild people who live scattered in pairs in the woods, than by the members of a vast, well-organized nation, having marvelously elaborated arts, extensive and profound knowledge, and multitudinous appliances to welfare?" The answer to this question will best be conveyed by an analogy.

As carried on throughout the animate world at large, the struggle for existence has been an indispensable means to evolution. Not simply do we see that, in the competition among individuals of the same kind, survival of the fittest has from the beginning furthered production of a higher type, but we see that to the unceasing warfare between species are mainly due both growth and organization. Without universal conflict there would have been no development of the active powers. The organs of perception and of locomotion have been little by little evolved during the interaction of pursuers and pursued. Improved limbs and senses have furnished better supplies to the viscera, and improved visceral structures have insured a better supply of aerated blood to the limbs and senses; while a higher nervous system has at each stage been required for duly coordinating the actions of these more complex structures. Among predatory animals death by starvation and among animals preyed upon death by destruction have carried off the least favorably modified individuals and varieties. Every advance in strength, speed, agility, or sagacity in creatures of the one class, has necessitated a corresponding advance in creatures of the other class; and without never-ending efforts to catch and to escape, with loss of life as the penalty for failure, the progress of neither could have been achieved.

Mark now, however, that while this merciless discipline of nature, "red in tooth and claw," has been essential to the evolution of sentient life, its persistence through all time with all creatures must not be inferred. The high organization evolved by and for this universal conflict is not necessarily for ever employed to like ends: the resulting power and intelligence admit of being far otherwise employed. Not for offense and defense only are the inherited structures useful, but for various other purposes; and these various other purposes may finally become the exclusive purposes. The myriads of years of warfare which have developed the powers of all lower types of creatures have bequeathed to the highest type of creature the powers now used by him for countless objects besides those of killing and avoiding being killed. His teeth and nails are but little employed in fight; and his mind is not ordinarily occupied in devising ways of destroying other creatures, or guarding himself from injury by them.

Similarly with social organisms. We must recognize the truth that the struggle for existence between societies has been instrumental to their evolution. Neither the consolidation and reconsolidation of small social groups into large ones, nor the organization of such compound and doubly compound groups, nor the concomitant developments of all those aids to a wider and higher life which civilization has brought, would have been possible without intertribal and international conflicts. Social cooperation is initiated by joint defense and offense; and from the cooperation thus initiated all kinds of cooperations have arisen. Inconceivable as have been the horrors caused by this universal antagonism which, beginning with the chronic hostilities of small hordes tens of thousands of years ago, has ended in the occasional vast battles of immense nations, we must nevertheless admit that without them the world would still have been inhabited only by men of feeble types, sheltering in caves and living on wild food.

But now observe that the intersocial struggle for existence which has been indispensable in evolving societies will not necessarily play in the future a part like that which it has played in the past. Recognizing our indebtedness to war for forming great communities and developing their structures, we may yet infer that the acquired powers, available for other activities, will lose their original activities. While conceding that without these perpetual bloody strifes civilized societies could not have arisen, and that an adapted form of human nature, fierce as well as intelligent, was a needful concomitant, we may at the same time hold that, such societies having been produced, the brutality of nature in their units which was necessitated by the process, ceasing to be necessary with the cessation of the process, will disappear. While the benefits achieved during the predatory period remain a permanent inheritance, the evils, social and individual, entailed by it will decrease and slowly die out.

Thus, then, contemplating social structures and actions from the evolution point of view, we may preserve that calmness which is needful for scientific interpretation of them, without losing our powers of feeling moral reprobation or approbation.

To these preliminary remarks respecting the mental attitude to be preserved by the student of political institutions, a few briefer ones must be added respecting the subject-matters he has to deal with.

If societies were all of the same species, and differed only in their stages of growth and structure, comparisons would disclose clearly the course of evolution; but unlikenesses of type among them, here great and there small, obscure the results of such comparisons.

Again, if each society grew and unfolded itself without the intrusion of additional factors, interpretation would be relatively easy; but the complicated processes of development are frequently recomplicated by sudden changes in the sets of factors. Now the size of the social aggregate is all at once increased or decreased by annexation or by loss of territory; and now the average character of its units is changed by the coming in of another race as conquerors or as slaves; while, as a further incident of this change, new social relations are superposed on the old. In many cases, the repeated overrunnings of societies by one another, the minglings of peoples and institutions, the breakings up and reaggregations, so destroy the continuity of normal changes as to make it extremely difficult if not impossible to draw conclusions.

Once more, change in the average mode of life pursued by a society, now increasingly warlike and now increasingly industrial, initiates metamorphoses: changed activities generate changes of structures. Hence, there have to be distinguished those progressive rearrangements which belong to the further development of one social type, from those caused by the commencing development of another social type. The lines of an organization adapted to a mode of activity that has ceased,

19

or has been long suspended, begin to fade, and are traversed by the increasingly definite lines of an organization adapted to the mode of activity which has replaced it; and error may result from mistaking traits which belong to the one for those which belong to the other.

Hence we may infer that, out of the complex and confused evidence, only the larger truths are likely to emerge with clearness. While anticipating that certain general conclusions are to be positively established, we may anticipate that more special ones can be alleged only as probable.

Happily, however, as we shall eventually see, those general conclusions admitting of positive establishment are the conclusions of most value for guidance.

II. Political Organization in General

The mere gathering of individuals into a group does not constitute them a society. A society, in the sociological sense, is formed only when, besides juxtaposition, there is cooperation. So long as members of the group do not combine their energies to achieve some common end or ends, there is little to keep them together. They are prevented from separating only when the wants of each are better satisfied by uniting his efforts with those of others than they would be if he acted alone.

Cooperation, then, is at once that which cannot exist without a society, and that for which a society exists. It may be a joining of many strengths to effect something which the strength of no single man can effect; or it may be an apportioning of different activities to different persons, who severally participate in the benefits of one another's activities. The motive for acting together, originally the dominant one, may be defense against enemies; or it may be the easier obtainment of food, by the chase or otherwise; or it may be, and commonly is, both of these. In any case, however, the units pass from the state of perfect independence to the state of mutual dependence; and as fast as they do this they become united into a society rightly so called.

But cooperation implies organization. If acts are to be effectually combined, there must be arrangements under which they are adjusted in their times, amounts, and characters.

This social organization, necessary as a means to concerted action, is of two kinds. Though these two kinds generally coexist, and are more or less interfused, yet they are distinct in their origins and natures. There is a spontaneous cooperation which grows up without thought during the pursuit of private ends; and there is a cooperation which, consciously devised, implies distinct recognition of public ends. The ways in which the two are respectively established and carried on present marked contrasts.

Whenever, in a primitive group, there begins that cooperation which is effected by exchange of services—whenever individuals find their wants better satisfied by giving certain products which they can make best in return for other products they are less skilled in making, or not so well circumstanced for making—there is initiated a kind of organization which then, and throughout its higher stages, results from endeavors to meet personal needs. The division of labor, to the last as at first, grows by experience of mutual facilitations in living. Each new specialization of industry arises from the effort of one who commences it to get profit, and establishes itself by conducing in some way to the profit of others. So that there is a kind of concerted action, with the elaborate social organization developed by it, which does not originate in deliberate concert. Though it is true that within the small subdivisions of this organization we find everywhere repeated the relation of employer and employed, of whom the one directs the actions of the other; yet this relation, spontaneously formed in the pursuit of private ends and continued only at will, is not made with conscious reference to achievement of public ends: ordinarily these are not thought of. And though, for the regulating of trading activities, there eventually arise agencies serving to adjust the supplies of commodities to the demands; yet such agencies do this not by direct stimulations or restraints, but simply by communicating information which serves to stimulate or restrain; and, further, these agencies themselves grow up not for the intended purpose of thus regulating, but in the pursuit of gain by individuals. So unintentionally has there arisen the elaborate division of labor by which production and distribution are now carried on, that only in modern days has there come a recognition of the fact that it has all along been arising.

On the other hand, that cooperation which unites the actions of individuals for a purpose immediately concerning the whole society, is a conscious cooperation, and is carried on by an organization of another kind, arising in a different way. When the primitive group has to defend itself against other groups, its members act together under further stimuli than those constituted by purely personal desires. Even at the outset, before any control by a chief exists, there is the control exercised by the group over its members; each of whom is obliged, by the *consensus* of opinion, to join in the general defense. Very soon the warrior of recognized superiority begins to exercise over each, during war, an influence additional to that exercised by the opinion of the group; and, when his authority becomes established, it greatly furthers combined action. From the beginning, therefore, this kind of social cooperation is a conscious cooperation, and a cooperation which is not wholly a matter of choice—is often much at variance with private wishes. As the organization initiated by it develops, we see that, in the first place, the fighting division of the society displays in a more marked degree these same traits; the grades and divisions constituting an army cooperate more and more under a regulation, consciously established, of agencies which override individual volitions—or, to speak strictly, control individuals by motives which prevent them from acting as they would spontaneously act. In the second place, we see that, throughout the society as a whole, there spreads a kindred form of organization— kindred in so far that, for the purpose of maintaining the militant organization and the government which directs it, there are similarly established over citizens agencies which force them to labor more or less largely for public ends instead of private ends. And, simultaneously, there develops a further organization, still akin in its fundamental principle, which restrains individual activities in such wise that social safety shall not be endangered by the disorder consequent on unchecked pursuit of personal ends. So that this kind of social organization is distinguished from the other, as arising through conscious pursuit of public ends, in furtherance of which individual wills are constrained, first of all by the joint wills of the entire group, and afterward more definitely by the will of a regulative agency which the group evolves.

Most clearly shall we perceive the contrast between these two kinds of organization on observing that, while they are both instrumental to social welfare, they are instrumental in converse ways. That organization shown us by the division of labor for industrial purposes exhibits combined action; but it is a combined action which directly seeks and subserves the welfares of individuals, and indirectly subserves the welfare of society as a whole by preserving individuals. Conversely, that kind of organization evolved for governmental and defensive purposes exhibits combined action; but it is a combined action which directly seeks and subserves the welfare of the society as a whole, and indirectly subserves the welfares of individuals by preserving the society. Efforts for self-preservation by the units originate the one form of organization; while efforts for self-preservation by the aggregate originate the other form of organization. In the one case there is conscious pursuit of private ends only; and the correlative organization resulting from this pursuit of private ends, growing up unconsciously, is without coercive power. In the other case there is conscious pursuit of public ends; and the correlative organization, consciously established, exercises coercion.

Of these two kinds of cooperation and the structures effecting them, we are here concerned only with one. Political organization is to be understood as that part of social organization which consciously carries on directive and restraining functions for public ends. It is true, as already hinted, and as we shall see presently, that the two kinds are mingled in various ways—that each ramifies through the other more or less according to their respective degrees of predominance. But the two are essentially different in origin and nature; and for the present we must, so far as may be, limit our attention to the last.

That the cooperation into which men have gradually risen secures to them benefits which could not be secured while, in their primitive state, they acted singly, and that, as an indispensable means to this cooperation, political organization has been, and is, advantageous, we shall see on contrasting the states of men who are not politically organized with the states of men who are politically organized in less or greater degrees.

There are, indeed, conditions under which as good an individual life is possible without political organization as with it. Where, as in the habitat of the Esquimaux, there are but few persons, and these very widely scattered; where there is no war, probably because the physical impediments to it are great and the motives to it feeble; and where circumstances make the occupations so uniform that there is little scope for the division of labor—mutual dependence can have no place, and the arrangements which effect it are not needed. Recognizing this exceptional case, let us consider the cases which are not exceptional.

The Digger Indians, "very few degrees removed from the orangoutang," who, scattered among the mountains of the Sierra Nevada, sheltering in holes and living on roots and vermin, "drag out a miserable existence in a state of nature, amid the most loathsome and disgusting squalor," differ from the other divisions of the Shoshones by their entire lack of social organization. The river-haunting and plain haunting divisions of the race, under some, though but slight, governmental control, lead more satisfactory lives. In South America the Chaco Indians, low in type as are the Diggers, and like them degraded and wretched in their lives, are similarly contrasted with the superior and more comfortable savages around them in being dissociated. Among the Bedouin tribes, the Sherarat are unlike the rest in being divided and subdivided into countless bands which have no common chief; and they are described as being the most miserable of the Bedouins. More decided still is the contrast noted by Baker between certain adjacent African peoples. Passing suddenly, he says, from the unclothed, ungoverned tribes—from the "wildest savagedom to semi-civilization"—we come in Unyoro to a country governed by "an unflinching despot," inflicting "death or torture" for "the most trivial offenses"; but where they have

25

developed administration, sub-governors, taxes, good clothing, arts, agriculture, architecture. So, too, concerning New Zealand when first discovered. Cook remarks that there seemed to be greater prosperity and populousness in the regions subject to a king.

These last cases introduce us to a further truth. Not only does that first step in political organization which places individuals under the control of a tribal chief bring the advantages gained by better cooperation, but such advantages are increased when minor political heads become subject to a major political head. As typifying the evils which are thereby avoided, I may name the fact that among the Belooches, whose tribes, unsubordinated to a general ruler, are constantly at war with one another, it is the habit to erect a small mud tower in each field, where the possessor and his retainers guard his produce—a state of things allied to, but worse than, that of the Highland clans, with their strongholds for sheltering women and cattle from the inroads of their neighbors, in days when they were not under the control of a central power. The benefits derived from such wider control, whether of a simple head or of a compound head, were felt by the early Greeks when the Amphictyonic Council established the laws that "no Hellenic tribe is to lay the habitations of another level with the ground; and from no Hellenic city is the water to be cut off during a siege." The good which results from that advance of political structure which unites smaller communities into larger ones was shown in our own country when, by the Roman conquest, the incessant fights between tribes were stopped; and again, in later days, when feudal nobles, becoming subject to a monarch, were debarred from private wars. Under its converse aspect, we see the same truth when, amid the anarchy which followed the collapse of the Carlovingian empire, princes and barons, resuming their independence, became active enemies to one another: their state being such that "when they were not at war they lived by open plunder." And the history of Europe has repeatedly, in many places and times, furnished kindred illustrations.

While political organization, as it extends itself throughout masses of increasing size, directly furthers welfare by removing that impediment to cooperation which the antagonism of individuals and of tribes causes, it indirectly furthers it in another way. Nothing beyond a rudimentary division of labor can arise in a small social group. Before commodities can be multiplied in their kinds, there must be multiplier! kinds of producers; and, before each commodity can be produced in the most economical way, the different stages in the production of it must be apportioned out among special hands. Nor is this all. Neither the required complex combinations of individuals, nor the elaborate mechanical appliances which facilitate manufacture, can arise in the absence of a large community, generating a great demand.

But though the advantages gained by cooperation presuppose political organization, this political organization necessitates disadvantages; and it is quite possible for these disadvantages to outweigh the advantages. The controlling structures have to be maintained, and the restraints they impose have to be borne; and the evils inflicted by taxation and by tyranny may become greater than the evils prevented.

Where, as in the East, the rapacity of monarchs has sometimes gone to the extent of taking from cultivators so much of their produce as to have afterward to return part for seed, we see exemplified the truth that the agency which maintains order may cause miseries greater than the miseries caused by disorder. The state of Egypt under the Romans, who, on the native set of officials, superposed their own set, and who made drafts on the country's resources not for local administration only but also for imperial administration, furnishes an instance. Beyond the regular taxes there were demands for feeding and clothing the military, wherever quartered; extra calls were continually made on the people for maintaining public works and subaltern agents; men in office were themselves so impoverished by exactions that they "assumed dishonorable employments or became the slaves of persons in power; gifts made to the government were soon converted into forced contributions; and those who purchased immunities from extortions found them disregarded as soon as the sums asked had been received. More marked still were the curses following excessive development of political organization in Gaul during the decline of the Roman Empire:

So numerous were the receivers in comparison with the payers, and so enormous the weight of taxation, that the laborer broke down, the plains became deserts, and woods grew where the plow had been. . . . It were impossible to number the officials who were rained upon every province and town. . . . The crack of the lash and the cry of the tortured filled the air. The faithful slave was tortured for evidence against his master, the wife to depose against her husband, the son against his sire. . . . Not satisfied with the returns of the first enumerators, they sent a succession of others, who each swelled the valuation—as a proof of service done; and so the imposts went on increasing. Yet the number of cattle fell off, and the people died. Nevertheless, the survivors had to pay the taxes of the dead.

And how literally in this case the benefits were exceeded by the mischiefs is shown by the remark that "they fear the enemy less than the tax-gatherer: the truth is, that they fly to the first to avoid the last. Hence, the one unanimous wish of the Roman populace, that it was their lot to live with the barbarian."

In the same regions during later times the lesson was repeated. While internal peace and its blessings were achieved in mediæval France as fast as feudal nobles became subordinate to the king—while the central power, as it grew stronger, put an end to that primitive practice of a blood-revenge which wreaked itself on any relative of an offender, and made the "truce of God" a needful mitigation of the universal savagery; yet from this extension of political organization there presently grew up evils as great or greater—multiplication of taxes, forced loans, groundless confiscations, arbitrary fines, progressive debasements of coinage, and a universal corruption of justice consequent on the sale of offices: the results being that many people died by famine, some committed suicide, while others, deserting their homes, led a wandering life. And then, afterward, when the supreme ruler, becoming absolute, controlled social life in all its details, through an administrative system vast in extent and ramifications, with the general result that in less than two centuries the indirect taxation alone "crossed the enormous interval between eleven millions and three hundred and eleven millions," there came the national impoverishment and misery which resulted in the great Revolution.

Even the present time supplies kindred evidence, in sundry places. A voyage up the Nile shows every observer that the people are better off where they are remote from the center of government—where administrative agencies can not so easily reach them. Nor is it only under the barbaric Turk that this happens. Notwithstanding the boasted beneficence of our rule in India, the extra burdens and the complication of restraints it involves have the effect that the people find some of the adjacent countries preferable; the ryots in sundry places are leaving their homes and settling in the territory of the Nizam and in Gwalior.

Not only do those who are controlled suffer, from political organization, evils which greatly deduct from, and sometimes exceed, the benefits. Numerous and rigid governmental restraints shackle those who impose them as well as those on whom they are imposed. The successive grades of ruling agents, severally coercing grades below, are themselves coerced by grades above; and even the very highest ruling agent is enslaved by the system created for the preservation of his supremacy. In ancient Egypt the daily life of the king was minutely regulated alike as to its hours, its occupations, its ceremonies; so that, nominally all-powerful, he was really less free than a subject. It has been, and is, the same with other despotic monarchs. Till lately, in Japan, where the form of organization had become fixed, and where, from the highest to the lowest, the actions of life were prescribed in detail, the exercise of authority was so burdensome that voluntary resignation of it was frequent. Adams writes, "The custom of abdication is common among all classes, from the Emperor down to his meanest subject." European states have examplified this reacting tyranny. "In the Byzantine palace," says Gibbon, "the Emperor was the first slave of the ceremonies he imposed." Concerning the tedious court life of Louis le Grand, Madame de Maintenon remarks: "Save those only who fill the highest stations, I know of none more unfortunate than those who envy them. If you could only form an idea of what it is!"

So that, while the satisfaction of men's personal wants is furthered both by the maintenance of order and by the formation of aggregates large enough to permit extensive division of labor, it is hindered both by deductions, often very great, from the products of their actions, and by the restraints imposed on their actions, usually in excess of the needs. And political control indirectly entails evils on those who exercise it as well as on those over whom it is exercised.

The stones composing a house cannot be otherwise used until the house has been pulled down. If the stones are united by mortar, there must be extra trouble in destroying their present combination before they can be recombined. And if the mortar has had centuries in which to consolidate, the breaking up of the masses formed is a matter of such difficulty that building with new materials becomes more economical than rebuilding with the old.

I name these facts to illustrate the truth that any kind of arrangement stands in the way of rearrangement; and that this must be true of organization, which is one kind of arrangement. When, during the evolution of a living body, its component substance, at first relatively homogeneous, has been transformed into a combination of heterogeneous parts, there results an obstacle, always great and often insuperable, to any considerable change of structure; the more elaborate and definite the structure the greater is the resistance it opposes to alteration. And this, which is conspicuously true of an individual organism, is true, if less conspicuously, of a social organism. Though a society, composed of discrete units, and

30

not having had its type fixed by inheritance from countless like societies, is much more plastic, yet the same principle holds. As fast as its parts are differentiated—as fast as there arise classes, bodies of functionaries, established institutions—these, becoming coherent within themselves and with one another, resist such forces as tend to modify them. The conservatism of every long-settled institution daily exemplifies this law. Be it in the antagonism of a Church to legislation interfering with its arrangements; be it in the opposition of an army to abolition of the purchase system; be it in the disfavor with which the legal profession at large has regarded law reform—we see that neither in their structures nor in their modes of action are parts that have once been specialized easily changed.

As it is true of a living body that its various acts have as their common end self-preservation, so is it true of its component organs that they severally tend to maintain themselves in their integrity. And, similarly, as it is true of a society that maintenance of its existence is the aim of its combined actions, so it is true of its separate classes and systems of officials, or other specialized parts, that the dominant aim of each is to preserve itself. Not the function to be performed, but the sustentation of those who perform the function, becomes the object in view: the result being that when the function is needless, or even detrimental, the structure still preserves itself as long as it can. In early days the history of the Knights Templars furnished an illustration of this tendency. Down to the present time we have before us the familiar instance of trade guilds in London, which, having ceased to perform their original functions, nevertheless jealously maintain themselves for no purpose but the gratification of their members. And the accounts given in "The Black-book," of the sinecures which survived up to recent times, yield multitudinous illustrations.

The extent to which an organization resists reorganization we shall not fully appreciate until we observe that its resistance increases in a compound progression. For, while each new part

31

is an additional obstacle to change, the formation of it implies a deduction from the forces causing change. If, other things remaining the same, the political structures of a society are further developed—if the existing institutions are extended or fresh ones set up—if, for directing social activities in greater detail, extra staffs of officials are appointed, the simultaneous results are an increase in the aggregate of those who form the regulating part and a corresponding decrease in the aggregate of those who form the part regulated. In various ways all who compose the controlling and administrative organization become united with one another and separated from the rest. Whatever be their particular duties, they are similarly related to the minor and major governing centers of their departments, and, through them, to the supreme governing center; and are habituated to like sentiments and ideas respecting the set of institutions in which they are incorporated. Receiving their subsistence through the national revenue, they tend toward kindred views and feelings respecting the raising of such revenue. Whatever jealousies there may be between their divisions, are overridden by sympathy when any one division has its existence or privileges endangered, since the interference with one division may spread to others. Moreover, they all stand in like relations to the rest of the community, whose actions are in one way or other superintended by them; and hence are led into kindred views respecting the need for such superintendence and the propriety of submitting to it. No matter what their previous political opinions may have been, they cannot become public agents of any kind without being biased toward opinions congruous with their functions. So that, inevitably, each further growth of the instrumentalities which control, or administer, or inspect, or in any way direct social forces, increases the impediment to future modifications, both positively, by strengthening that which has to be modified, and negatively, by weakening the remainder; until at length the rigidity becomes so great that change is impossible and the type becomes fixed.

Nor does each further development of the regulative organization increase the obstacles to change only by relatively increasing the power of those who, as regulators, maintain the established order, and decreasing the power of those who, as the regulated, have not the same direct interests in maintaining it. For the ideas and sentiments of a community as a whole progressively adapt themselves to the *régime* familiar from childhood, in such wise that it comes to be looked upon as natural, and as the only thing possible. In proportion as public agencies occupy a larger space in daily experience, leaving but a smaller space for other agencies, there comes a greater tendency to think of public control as everywhere needful, and a less ability to conceive of activities as otherwise controlled. At the same time the sentiments, adjusted by habit to the regulative machinery, become enlisted on its behalf, and adverse to the thought of a vacancy to be made by its absence. In brief, the general law, that the social organism and its units act and react in such ways as to become congruous, implies that every further extension of political organization increases the obstacle to reorganization, not only by increasing the strength of the regulative part and decreasing the strength of the part regulated, but also by producing in citizens thoughts and feelings in harmony with the resulting structure, and out of harmony with anything substantially different. Both France and Germany furnish examples of this truth. M. Comte, while looking forward to an industrial state, was so swayed by the ideas and sentiments appropriate to the French form of society, that his scheme of organization for the industrial state prescribes its arrangements with a definiteness and detail characteristic of the militant type, and utterly at variance with the industrial type. Indeed, he had a profound aversion to that individualism which is a product of industrial life and gives the character to industrial institutions. So, too, in Germany, we see that the Socialist party, who are regarded and who regard themselves as wishing to entirely reorganize society, are so incapable of really thinking away from the social type under which they have been born and nurtured, that their proposed social system is in essence nothing else than a new form of the system they would destroy. It is a system under which life and labor are to be arranged and superintended by public instrumentalities, omnipresent like those which already exist and no less coercive, the individual having his life even more regulated for him than now.

While, then, on the one hand, in the absence of settled arrangements, there can not be coöperation, yet coöperation of a higher kind is hindered by the arrangements which facilitate coöperation of a lower kind. Though, without some established relations among parts, there can be no combined actions, yet, the more extensive and elaborate such relations grow, the more difficult does it become to make an improved combination of actions. There is an increase of the forces which tend to fix, and a decrease of the forces which tend to unfix; until the fully-structured social organism, like fully-structured individual organism, becomes no longer adaptable.

In a living animal, formed as it is of aggregated units originally like in kind, the progress of organization implies, not only that the units composing each differentiated part severally maintain their positions, but also that their progeny succeed to those positions. Bile cells which, while performing their functions, grow and give origin to new bile-cells, are, when they decay and disappear, replaced by these: the cells descending from them do not migrate to the kidneys, or the muscles, or the nervous centers, to join in the performance of their duties. And, evidently, unless the specialized units each organ is made of gave origin to units similarly specialized, which remained in the same place, there could be none of those settled relations among parts which characterize the organism and fit it for its particular mode of life.

In a society, also, fixity of structure is favored by the transmission of positions and functions through successive generations. The maintenance of those class-divisions which arise as political organization advances implies the inheritance of a rank and a place in each class. Obviously, in proportion as the difficulty of rising from one grade into another is great, the social grades become settled in their relations. The like happens with those subdivisions of classes which, in some societies, constitute castes, and in other societies are partially exemplified by guilds. Where custom or law compels the sons of each trader to follow his father's occupation, there result, among the structures carrying on production and distribution, obstacles to change analogous to those which result in the regulative structures from impassable divisions of ranks. India shows this in an extreme degree; and in a less degree it was shown by the craft-guilds of early days in England, which facilitated adoption of a craft by the children of those engaged in it, and hindered adoption of it by others. Thus we may call inheritance of position and function the principle of fixity in social organization.

There is another way in which succession by inheritance, whether to class-position or to occupation, conduces to stability. It secures supremacy of the elder; and supremacy of the elder tends toward maintenance of the established order. A system under which a chief-ruler, sub-ruler, head of a clan or house, official, or any person having the power given by rank or property, has his place filled up at death by a descendant, in conformity with some accepted rule of succession, is a system under which, by implication, the young, and even the middle aged, are excluded from the conduct of affairs. So, too, where an industrial system is such that the son, habitually brought up to his father's business, succeeds to his position when he dies, it follows in like manner that the regulative power of the elder over the processes of production and distribution is scarcely at all qualified by the power of the younger. Now, it is a truth daily exemplified that increasing rigidity of organization, necessitated by the process of evolution, produces in age an increasing strength of habit and aversion to change. Hence it results that succession to place and function by inheritance, having as its necessary concomitant the monopoly of power by the eldest, involves a prevailing conservatism; and this further insures maintenance of things as they are.

Conversely, social change is facile in proportion as men's positions and functions are determinable by personal qualities. If, not being prevented by law or custom, members of one rank establish themselves in another rank, they in so far directly break the division between the ranks; and they indirectly weaken the division by preserving their family relations with the first, and forming new ones with the second; while, further, the ideas and sentiments prevailing in the two ranks, previously more or less different, are made to qualify one another and to modify the characters of their members. Similarly, if between subdivisions of the producing and distributing classes there are no barriers to migration, then, in proportion as migrations are numerous, influences physical and mental, following interfusion, tend to alter the natures of their units; at the same time that they perpetually check the establishment of differences of nature, caused by differences of function. Such transpositions of individuals between class and class, or group and group, must, on the average, however, be determined by the fitnesses of the individuals for their new places and duties. Intrusions will ordinarily succeed only where the intruding citizens have more than usual aptitudes for the businesses they undertake. Those who desert their original social positions and occupations are at a disadvantage in the competition with those whose positions and occupations they assume; and they can overcome this disadvantage only by force of some superiority in respect of the occupations in which they compete. This leaving of men to have their careers determined by their efficiencies we may therefore call the principle of change in social organization.

As we saw that succession by inheritance conduces in a secondary way to stability, by keeping the places of authority in the hands of those who by age are made most averse to new practices, so here, conversely, we may see that succession by efficiency conduces in a secondary way to change. Both positively and negatively the possession of power by the young facilitates innovation. While the energies are overflowing, little fear is felt of those obstacles to improvement and evils it may bring, which, to those of flagging energies, look formidable; and at the same time the greater imaginativeness that goes along with higher vitality, joined with a smaller strength of habit, facilitates acceptance of fresh ideas and adoption of untried methods. Since, then, where the various social positions come to be respectively filled by those who are experimentally proved to be the fittest, the relatively young are permitted to exercise authority, it results that succession by efficiency furthers change in social organization, indirectly as well as directly.

Contrasting the two, we thus see that, while the acquirement of function by inheritance conduces to rigidity of structure, the acquirement of function by efficiency conduces to plasticity of structure. Succession by descent favors the maintenance of that which exists. Succession by fitness favors transformation, and makes possible something better.

As previously pointed out, "complication of structure accompanies increase of mass," in social organisms as in individual organisms. When small societies are compounded into a larger society, the controlling agencies needed in the several component societies must be subordinated to a central controlling agency: new structures are required. Recompounding necessitates a kindred further complexity in the governmental arrangements; and at each of such stages of increase all other arrangements must become more complicated. As Duruy remarks: "By becoming a world in place of a town, Rome could not conserve institutions established for a single city and a small territory. . . . How was it possible for sixty millions of provincials to enter the narrow and rigid circle of provincial institutions?" The like holds where, instead of extension of territory, there is only increase of population. The contrast between the simple administrative system which sufficed in old English times for a million people and the complex administrative system at present needed for many millions sufficiently indicates this general truth.

But now, mark a corollary. If, on the one hand, further growth implies more complex structure, on the other hand changeableness of structure is a condition to further growth; and, conversely, unchangeableness of structure is a concomitant of arrested growth. Like the correlative law just noted, this law is clearly seen in individual organisms. On the one hand, the transition from the small immature form to the large mature form, in a living creature, implies that not the whole only, but all the parts have to be changed in their sizes and connections; every detail of every organ has to be modified; and this implies the retention of plasticity. On the other hand, when, on approaching maturity, the structures are assuming their final arrangement, their increasing definiteness and firmness constitute an increasing impediment to growth: the unbuilding and rebuilding required before there can be the needful readjustment become more and more difficult. So is it with a society. Augmentation of its mass necessitates change of the preexisting structures, either by incorporation of the increment with them, or by their extension through it. Every elaboration and further settlement of the structures presents an additional obstacle to this; and, when rigidity is reached, such modifications of them as increase of mass would involve are impossible, and increase is prevented.

Hence a significant relation between the structure of a society and its growth. While each increment of growth is aided by an appropriate organization, yet this organization, being inappropriate to a greater mass, becomes thereafter an impediment to further growth. Whence it follows that organization in excess of need prevents the attainment of that larger size and accompanying higher organization which might else have arisen.

To aid our interpretations of the special facts presently to be dealt with, we must keep in mind the foregoing general facts. They may be summed up as follows:

Cooperation is made possible by society, and makes society possible. It presupposes associated men, and men remain associated because of the benefits association yields them.

But there cannot be concerted actions without agencies by which actions are in some way adjusted in their times, amounts, and kinds; and the actions cannot be of various kinds without the cooperators undertaking different duties. That is to say, the cooperators must fall into some kind of organization, either voluntarily or involuntarily.

The organization which cooperation implies is of two kinds, distinct in origin and nature. The one, arising directly from the pursuit of individual ends and indirectly conducing to social welfare, develops unconsciously and is non-coercive. The other, arising directly from the pursuit of social ends and indirectly conducing to individual welfare, develops consciously and is coercive.

While, by making cooperation possible, political organization achieves benefits, deductions from the benefits are entailed by such organization. Maintenance of it is costly; and the cost may become a greater evil than the evils escaped. It necessarily imposes restraints; and these restraints may become so extreme that anarchy, with all its miseries, is preferable.

Organization as it becomes established is an obstacle to reorganization. Both by the inertia of position, and by the cohesion gradually established among them, the units of the structures formed oppose change. Self-sustentation is the primary aim of each part as of the whole; and hence parts once formed tend to continue, whether they are or are not useful. Moreover, each addition to the regulative structures implying, other things equal, a simultaneous deduction from the remainder of the society which is regulated, it results that, while the obstacles to change are increased, the forces causing change are decreased.

Maintenance of a society's organization implies that the units forming its component structures shall severally be replaced as they die. Stability is favored if the vacancies they leave are filled without dispute by descendants; while change is favored if the vacancies are filled by those who are experimentally proved to be best fitted for them. Succession by inheritance is thus the principle of social rigidity; while succession by efficiency is the principle of social plasticity.

Though to make cooperation possible, and therefore to facilitate social growth, there must be organization, yet the organization formed impedes further growth; since further growth implies reorganization, which the existing organization resists.

So that while, at each stage, better immediate results may be achieved by completing organization, they must be at the expense of better ultimate results. These are to be achieved by carrying organization at each stage no further than is needful for the orderly carrying on of social actions.

III. Political Integration

Political integration is in some cases furthered, and in other cases hindered, by conditions, external and internal. There are the characters of the environment, and there are the characters of the men composing the society. We will glance at them in this order.

How political integration is prevented by an inclemency of climate, or an infertility of soil, which keeps down population, has been already shown. To the instances before named may be added that of the Seminoles, of whom Schoolcraft says, "Being so thinly scattered over a barren desert, they seldom assemble to take black drink, or deliberate on public matters"; and, again, that of certain Snake Indians, of whom he says, "The paucity of game in this region is, I have little doubt, the cause of the almost entire absence of social organization." We saw, too, that great uniformity of surface, of mineral products, of flora, of fauna, are impediments; and that on the special characters of the flora and fauna, as containing species favorable or unfavorable to human welfare, in part depends the individual prosperity required for social growth. It was also pointed out that structure of the habitat, as facilitating or impeding communication, and as rendering escape easy or hard, has much to do with the size of the social aggregate formed. To the illustrations before given, showing that mountain-haunting peoples, and peoples living in deserts and marshes, are difficult to consolidate, while peoples penned in by barriers are consolidated with facility, I may here add two significant ones not yet noticed. One occurs in the Polynesian Islands—Tahiti, Hawaii, Tonga, Samoa, and the rest—where, restrained within limits by surrounding seas, the inhabitants have become united more or less closely into aggregates of considerable sizes. The other is furnished by ancient Peru, where, before the time of the Incas, semi-civilized communities had been formed in valleys separated from each

41

other "on the coast, by hot and almost impassable deserts, and in the interior by lofty mountains, or cold and trackless *punas*." And to the implied inability of these peoples to escape governmental coercion, thus indicated by Squier as a factor in their civilization, is ascribed, by the ancient Spanish writer Cieza, the difference between them and the neighboring Indians of Popayan, who could retreat, "whenever attacked, to other fertile regions." How, conversely, within the area occupied, the massing of men together is furthered by ease of internal communication, is sufficiently manifest. The importance of it is implied by the remark of Grant concerning equatorial Africa, that "no jurisdiction extends over a district which cannot be crossed in three or four days." And such facts, implying that political integration may increase as the means of going from place to place become better, remind us how, from Roman times downward, the formation of roads has made larger social aggregates possible.

Evidence that a certain type of *physique* is requisite has been elsewhere given. We saw that the races which have proved capable of evolving large societies have been races previously subject, for long periods, to conditions fostering vigor of constitution. I will here add only that the constitutional energy needed for continuous labor, without which there cannot be civilized life and the massing of men that accompanies it, is an energy not to be quickly acquired under any conditions or through any discipline, but to be acquired only by inherited modifications slowly accumulated. Good evidence that in lower types of men there is a physical incapacity for continuous labor, is supplied by the results of the Jesuit government over the Paraguay Indians. These Indians were reduced to industrial habits, and to an orderly life which was thought by many writers admirable; but there eventually resulted the fatal evil that they became infertile. Not improbably, the infertility habitually observed in savage races that have been led into civilized habits, is consequent on taxing the *physique* to a degree greater than it is constituted to bear.

Certain moral traits which favor, and others which hinder, the union of men into large groups, were pointed out when treating of "The Primitive Man—Emotional." Here I will reillustrate such of these as concern the fitness or unfitness of the type for subordination, "The Abors, as they themselves say, are like tigers, two can not dwell in one den," writes Mr. Dalton; and "their houses are scattered singly, or in groups of two and three." Conversely, some of the African races not only yield when coerced, but admire one who coerces them; instance the Damaras, who, as Galton says, "court slavery" and "follow a master as spaniels would." The like is alleged of other South Africans. One of them said to a gentleman known to me: "You're a pretty fellow to be a master; I've been with you two years and you've never beaten me once." Obviously the dispositions thus strongly contrasted are dispositions on which the impossibility or possibility of political integration largely depends. There must be added, as also influential, the presence or the absence of the nomadic instinct. Varieties of men, in whom wandering habits have been unchecked during countless generations of hunting life and pastoral life, show us that, even when forced into agricultural life, their tendency to move about greatly hinders aggregation. It is thus among the hill-tribes of India. "The Kookies are naturally a migratory race, never occupying the same place for more than two or, at the utmost, three years"; and the like holds of the Mishmees, who "never name their villages"—the existence of them being too transitory. In some races this migratory instinct survives and shows its effects, even after the formation of populous towns. Writing of the Bachassins in 1812, Burchell says that Litakun, containing 15,000 inhabitants, had been twice removed during a period of ten years. Clearly, people so little attached to the localities they were born in are not so easily united into large societies as people who love their early homes.

Concerning the intellectual traits which aid or impede the cohesion of men into masses, I may supplement what was said when delineating "The Primitive Man—Intellectual," by two corollaries of much significance. Social life, being coöperative life, presupposes not only an emotional nature fitted for coöperation, but also such. intelligence as perceives the benefits of coöperation, and can so regulate actions as to effect it. The unreflectiveness, the deficient consciousness of causation, and the utter lack of constructive imagination, shown by the uncivilized, hinder coöperation to a degree difficult to believe until proof is seen. Even the semi-civilized exhibit in quite simple matters an absence of concert which is astonishing. Implying, as this inaptitude does, that coöperation can at first be effective only where there is obedience to peremptory command, it follows that there must be not only an emotional nature which produces subordination, but also an intellectual nature which produces faith in a commander. That credulity which leads to awe of the capable man, as a possessor of supernatural power, and which afterward, causing dread of his ghost, prompts fulfillment of his remembered injunctions—that credulity which initiates the religious control of a deified chief, reenforcing the control of his divine descendant—is a credulity which cannot be dispensed with during early stages of integration. Skepticism is fatal while the character, moral and intellectual, is such as to necessitate compulsory cooperation.

Political integration, then, hindered in many regions by environing conditions, has, in many races of mankind, been prevented from advancing far by unfitnesses of nature— physical, moral, and intellectual.

Besides certain fitnesses of nature in the united individuals, social union requires a considerable likeness of kind in their natures. At the outset the likeness of kind is insured by greater or less kinship in blood. Evidence of this meets us everywhere among the uncivilized. Of the Bushmen, Lichtenstein says: "Families alone form associations in single small hordes; sexual feelings, the instinctive love to children, or the customary attachment among relations, are the only ties that keep them in any sort of union." Again, "The Rock Veddahs are divided into small clans or families associated for

44

relationship, who agree in partitioning the forest among themselves for hunting-grounds," etc. And this rise of the society out of the family, seen in these least organized groups, reappears in the considerably organized groups of more advanced savages. Instance the New-Zealanders, of whom we read that "eighteen historical nations occupy the country, each being subdivided into many tribes, originally families, as the prefix Ngati, signifying offspring (equivalent to O or Mac), obviously indicates." This connection between blood-relationship and social union is well shown by Humboldt's remarks concerning South American Indians. "Savages," he says, "know only their own family, and a tribe appears to them but a more numerous assemblage of relations." When Indians who inhabit the missions see those of the forest, who are unknown to them, they say: "They are, no doubt, my relations; I understand them when they speak to me." But these very savages detest all who are not of their family or their tribe; "they know the duties of family ties and of relationship, but not those of humanity."

When treating of the domestic relations, reasons were given for concluding that social stability increases as kinships become more definite and extended; since development of kinships, while insuring the likeness of nature which furthers cooperation, involves the strengthening and multiplication of those family bonds which check disruption. Where promiscuity is prevalent, or where marriages are temporary, the known relationships are relatively few and not close; and there is little more social cohesion than results from belonging to the same type of man. Polyandry, especially of the higher kind, produces relationships of some definiteness, which admit of being traced further; so serving better to tie the social group together. And a greater advance in the nearness and the number of family connections results from polygyny. But, as was shown, it is from monogamy that there arise family connections which are at once the most definite and the most wide spreading in their ramifications; and out of monogamic families are developed the largest and most coherent societies.

In two allied yet distinguishable ways does monogamy favor social solidarity.

Unlike the children of the polyandrous family, who are something less than half brothers and sisters, and unlike the children of the polygamous family, most of whom are only half brothers and sisters, the children of the monogamous family are, in the great majority of cases, all of the same blood on both sides. Being thus themselves more closely related, it follows that their clusters of children are more closely related; and where, as happens in early stages, these clusters of children when grown up continue to form a community, and labor together, they are united alike by their kinships arid by their industrial interests. Though with the growth of a family group into a gens which spreads, the industrial interests divide, yet these kinships prevent the divisions from becoming as marked as they would otherwise become. And, similarly, when the *gens,* in course of time, develops into the tribe. Nor is this all. If local circumstances bring together several such tribes, which are still allied in blood, though more remotely, it results that when, seated side by side, they are gradually fused, partly by interspersion and partly by intermarriage, the compound society formed, united by numerous and complicated links of kinship as well as by political interests, is more strongly bound together than it would otherwise be. Dominant ancient societies illustrate this truth. Says Grote: "All that we hear of the most ancient Athenian laws is based upon the gentile and phratric divisions, which are treated throughout as extensions of the family." Similarly, according to Mommsen, on the "Roman household was based the Roman state, both as respected its constituent elements and its form. The community of the Roman people arose out of the junction (in whatever way brought about) of such ancient clanships as the Romilii, Voltinii, Fabii, etc." And Sir Henry Maine has shown in detail the ways in which the simple family passes into the house community, and eventually the village community. Though, in presence of the evidence furnished by races having irregular sexual relations, we cannot allege that sameness of blood is the primary reason for political cooperation—though in numerous tribes which have not risen into the pastoral state, there is combination for offense and defense among those whose names are recognized marks of different bloods—yet where there has been established descent through males, and especially where monogamy prevails, sameness of blood becomes largely, if not mainly, influential in determining political cooperation. And this truth, under one of its aspects, is the truth above enunciated, that combined action, requiring a certain likeness of nature among those who carry it on, is, in early stages, most successful among those who, being descendants of the same ancestors, have the greatest likeness.

An all-important though less direct effect of blood-relationship, and especially that more definite blood-relationship which arises from monogamic marriage, has to be added. I mean community of religion—a likeness of ideas and sentiments embodied in the worship of a comman deity. Beginning, as this does, with the propitiation of the deceased founder of the family, and shared in, as it is, by the multiplying groups of descendants, as the family spreads, it becomes a further means of holding together the compound cluster gradually formed, and checking the antagonisms that arise between the component clusters: so favoring integration. The influence of the bond supplied by a common cult everywhere meets us in ancient history. Each of the cities in primitive Egypt was a center for the worship of a special divinity; and no one who, unbiased by foregone conclusions, observes the extraordinary development of ancestor-worship, under all its forms, in Egypt, can doubt the origin of this divinity. Of the Greeks we read that "each family had its own sacred rites and funereal commemoration of ancestors, celebrated by the master of the house, to which none but members of the family were admissible: the extinction of a family, carrying with it the suspension of these religious rites, was held by the Greeks to be a misfortune, not merely from the loss of the citizens composing it, but also because the family gods and the manes of deceased citizens were thus deprived of their honors and might visit the country with displeasure. The larger associations, called Gens, Phratry, Tribe, were formed by an extension of the same principle—of the family considered as a religious brotherhood, worshiping some common god or hero with an appropriate surname, and recognizing him as their joint ancestor."

A like bond was generated in a like manner in the Roman community. Each curia, which was the homologue of the phratry, had a head, "whose chief function was to preside over the sacrifices." And, on a larger scale, the same thing held with the entire society. The primitive Roman king was a priest of the deities common to all; "he held intercourse with the gods of the community, whom he consulted and whom he appeased." The beginnings of this religious bond, here exhibited in a developed form, are still traceable in India. Sir Henry Maine, says, "The joint family of the Hindoos is that assemblage of persons who would have joined in the sacrifices at the funeral of some common ancestor if he had died in their lifetime." So that political integration, while furthered by that likeness of nature which identity of descent involves, is again furthered by that likeness of religion simultaneously arising from this identity of descent.

Thus is it, too, at a later stage, with that less pronounced likeness of nature characterizing men of the same race who have multiplied and spread in such ways as to form adjacent small societies. Cooperation among them continues to be furthered, though less effectually, by the community of their natures, by the community of their traditions, ideas, and sentiments, as well as by their community of language. Among men of diverse types, cooperation is necessarily hindered not only by that absence of mutual comprehension caused by ignorance of one another's words, but also by unlikenesses in their ways of thinking and feeling. It needs but to remember how often, even among those who speak the same language, quarrels arise from misinterpretations of things said, to see what fertile sources of confusion and antagonism must be the partial or complete differences of speech which habitually accompany differences of race. Similarly, those who are widely unlike in their emotional natures, or in their intellectual natures, perplex one another by unexpected conduct—a fact on which travelers habitually remark. Hence a further obstacle to combined action. Diversities of custom, too, become causes of dissension. Where a food eaten by one people is regarded by another with disgust, where an animal held sacred by the one is by the other treated with contempt, where a salute which the one expects is never made by the other, there must be continually generated alienations which hinder joint efforts. Other things equal, facility of cooperation will be proportionate to the amount of fellow-feeling; the fellow-feeling is prevented by whatever prevents men from behaving in the same ways under the same conditions. The working together of the original and derived factors above enumerated is well exhibited in the following passage from Grote: "The Hellens were all of common blood and parentage—were all descendants of the common patriarch Hellen. In treating of the historical Greeks, we have to accept this as a datum: it represents the sentiment under the influence of which they moved and acted. It is placed by Herodotus in the front rank, as the chief of those four ties which bound together the Hellenic aggregate: 1. Fellowship of blood; 2. Fellowship of language; 3. Fixed domiciles of gods, and sacrifices common to all; 4. Like manners and dispositions."

Influential as we thus find to be the likeness of nature which is insured by common descent, the implication is that, in the absence of considerable likeness, the larger political aggregates formed are unstable, and can be maintained only by a coercion which, some time or other, is sure to fail. Though other causes have conspired, yet this has doubtless been a part cause of the dissolution of great empires in past ages. At the present time the decay of the Turkish Empire is largely if not chiefly ascribable to it. Our own Indian Empire, too, held together by force in a state of artificial equilibrium, threatens some day to illustrate, by its fall, the incohesion arising from lack of congruity in its components.

One of the laws of evolution at large is, that integration results when like units are subject to the same force or to like forces ("First Principles," § 169); and, from the first stages of political integration up to the last, we find this law illustrated. Joint exposure to uniform external actions and joint reactions against them have from the beginning been the leading causes of union among members of societies.

Already there has been indirectly implied the truth that coherence is first given to small hordes of primitive men during combined opposition to enemies. Subject to the same danger, and uniting to meet this danger, they become, in the course of their cooperation against it, more bound together. In the first stages, this relation of cause and effect is clearly seen in the fact that such union as arises during a war disappears when the war is over: there is dispersion and loss of all such slight political subordination as was beginning to show itself. But it is by the integration of simple groups into compound groups, in the course of common resistance to foes and attacks upon them, that this process is best exemplified. The cases before given may be reenforced by others. Of the Karens, Mason says: "Each village, being an independent community, had always an old feud to settle with nearly every other village among their own people. But the common danger from more powerful enemies, or having common injuries to requite, often led to several villages uniting together for defense or attack." According to Kolben, "smaller nations of Hottentots, which may be near some powerful nation, frequently enter into an alliance, offensive and defensive, against the stronger nation." Among the New Caledonians, in Tanna, "six, or eight, or more of their villages unite, and form what may be called a district, or county, and all league together for mutual protection. . . . In war, two or more of these districts unite." In Samoa, "villages, in numbers of eight or ten, unite by common consent, and form a district or state for mutual protection"; and, in time of war, these districts themselves sometimes unite in twos and threes. The like has happened with historic peoples. It was during the wars of the Israelites, in David's time, that they passed from the state of separate tribes into the state of a consolidated ruling nation. The scattered Greek communities, previously aggregated into minor confederacies by minor wars, were prompted to the Panhellenic congress and to the subsequent cooperation, when the invasion of Xerxes was impending; and, of the Spartan and Athenian confederacies afterward formed, that of Athens acquired the hegemony, and finally the empire, during continued operations against the Persians. So, too, was it with the Teutonic races. The German tribes, originally without federal bond, formed occasional alliances for war. Between the first and fifth centuries these tribes gradually massed into great groups for resistance against or attack upon Rome. During the subsequent century the prolonged military confederations of peoples "of the same blood" had become states. And afterward these became aggregated into still larger states. And, to take a comparatively modern instance, it was during the wars between France and England that each passed from that condition, in which its component feudal groups were in considerable degrees independent, to the condition of a consolidated nation. As further showing how integration of smaller societies into larger ones is thus initiated, it may be added that at first the unions exist only for military purposes: each component society retains for a long time its independent internal administration, and it is only when joint action in war has become habitual that the cohesion is made permanent by a common political organization.

This compounding of smaller communities into larger by military cooperation is insured by the disappearance of such smaller communities as do not cooperate. Barth remarks that "the Fúlbe [Fulahs] are continually advancing, as they have not to do with one strong enemy, but with a number of small tribes without any bond of union." Of the Damaras, Galton says: "If one werft is plundered, the adjacent ones rarely rise to defend it, and thus the Namaquas have destroyed or enslaved piecemeal about one half of the whole Damara population." Similarly, according to Ondegardo, with the Inca conquests in Peru: "There was no general opposition to their advance, for each province merely defended its land without aid from any other." This process, so obvious and familiar, I name because it has a meaning which needs emphasizing. For we here see that, in the struggle for existence among societies, the survival of the fittest is the survival of those in which the power of military cooperation is the greatest; and military cooperation is that primary kind of cooperation which prepares the way for other kinds of cooperation. So that this formation of larger societies by the union of smaller ones in war, and this destruction or absorption of the smaller ununited societies by the united larger ones, is an inevitable process through which the varieties of men most adapted for social life supplant the less adapted varieties.

Respecting the integration thus effected, it remains only to remark that it necessarily follows this course—necessarily begins with the formation of simple groups and advances by the compounding and the recompounding of these. Impulsive in conduct and with feeble powers of cooperation, savages cohere so slightly that only small bodies of them can maintain their integrity. Not until such small bodies have severally had their members bound to one another by some slight political organization does it become possible to unite them into larger bodies; since the cohesion of these implies greater fitness for concerted action, and more developed organization for achieving it. And, similarly, these composite clusters must be to some extent consolidated before the composition can be carried a stage further. Passing over the multitudinous illustrations occurring among the uncivilized, it will suffice if I refer to those given before, and reenforce them by some which historic peoples have supplied. There is the fact that in primitive Egypt the numerous small societies (which eventually became the "nomes") first united into the two aggregates. Upper Egypt and Lower Egypt, which were afterward joined into one; and the fact that, in ancient Greece, villages became united to adjacent towns before the towns became united into states, while this change preceded the change which united the states with one another; and the fact that, in the old English period, small principalities were massed into the divisions constituting the Heptarchy before these passed into something like a united whole. It is a principle in physics that, since the force with which a body resists strains increases only as the squares of its dimensions, while the strains which its own weight subject it to increase as the cubes of its dimensions, its power of maintaining its integrity becomes relatively less as its mass becomes greater. Something analogous may be said of societies. Small aggregates only can hold together while the cohesion is feeble, and successively larger aggregates become possible only as the greater strains implied are met by that greater cohesion which results from an adapted human nature, and a resulting development of social organization.

As social integration advances, the increasing aggregates exercise increasing restraints over their units—a truth which is the obverse of the one just set forth, that the maintenance of its integrity by a larger aggregate implies greater cohesion. The coercive forces by which aggregates keep their units together are at first very slight, and, becoming extreme at a certain stage of social evolution, afterward relax—or, rather, change their forms.

At the outset the individual savage gravitates to one group or other, prompted by sundry motives, but mainly by the desire for protection. Concerning the Patagonians, we read that no one can live apart: "If any of them attempted to do it, they would undoubtedly be killed, or carried away as slaves, as soon as they were discovered." In North America, among the Chinooks, "on the coast a custom prevails which authorizes the seizure and enslavement, unless ransomed by his friends, of every Indian met with at a distance from his tribe, although they may not be at war with each other." At first, however, though it is necessary to join some group, it is not necessary to continue in the same group. In early stages migrations from group to group are common. When much oppressed by their chief, Calmucks and Mongols desert him and go over to other chiefs. Of the Abipones, Dobrizhoffer says: "Without leave asked on their part, or displeasure evinced on his, they remove with their families whithersoever it suits them, and join some other cacique; and, when tired of the second, return with impunity to the horde of the first." Similarly, in South Africa, "the frequent instances which occur [among the Balonda] of people changing from one part of the country to another show that the great chiefs possess only a limited power." And how, through this process, some tribes grow while others dwindle, we are shown by McCulloch's remark respecting the Kukis, that "a village, having around it plenty of land suited for cultivation and a popular chief, is sure soon, by accessions from less favored ones, to become large."

With the need which the individual has for protection is joined the desire of the tribe to strengthen itself; and the practice of adoption, hence resulting, constitutes another mode of integration. Where, as among tribes of North American Indians, "adoption or the torture were the alternative chances of a captive" (adoption being the fate of one admired for his bravery), we see reillustrated the tendency which each society has to grow at the expense of other societies. That desire for many actual children whereby the family may be strengthened, which Hebrew traditions show us, readily passes into the desire for factitious children—here made one with the brotherhood by exchange of blood, and there by mock birth. As was implied in another place, it is probable that the practice of adoption into families so prevalent in Rome arose during those early times when the wandering patriarchal group constituted the tribe, and when the desire of the tribe to strengthen itself was dominant. And, indeed, on remembering that, long after larger societies were formed by the compounding of patriarchal groups, there continued to be feuds between the component families and clans, we may see that there had never ceased to operate, on such families and clans, the primitive motive for strengthening themselves by increasing their numbers.

It may be added that kindred motives produced kindred results within more modern societies, during times when their component parts were so imperfectly integrated that there remained antagonisms among them. Thus we have the fact that in mediæval England, while local rule was incompletely subordinated to general rule, every free man had to attach himself to a lord, a burgh, or a guild: being otherwise "a friendless man," and in a danger like that which the savage is in when not belonging to a tribe. And. then, on the other hand, in the law that, "if a bondsman continued a year and a day within a free burgh or municipality, no lord could reclaim him," we may recognize an effect of the desire on the part of industrial groups to strengthen themselves against the feudal groups around—an effect analogous to the adoption, here into the savage tribe and there into the family as it existed in the ancient societies. Naturally, as a whole nation becomes more completely integrated, these local integrations become weaker, and finally disappear; though they long leave their traces, as among ourselves even still in the law of settlement, and as, up to so late a period as 1824, in the laws affecting the freedom of traveling of artisans.

These last illustrations introduce us to the truth that, while at first there are little cohesion and great mobility of the units forming a group, advance in integration is habitually accompanied not only by a decreasing ability to go from group to group, but also by a decreasing ability to go from place to place with the group: the members of the society become less free to move about within the society as well as less free to leave it. Of course, the transition from the nomadic to the settled state partially implies this; since each person becomes in a considerable degree tied by his material interests. Slavery, too, effects in another way this binding of individuals to locally-placed members of the society, and therefore to particular parts to it; and, where serfdom exists, the same thing is shown with a difference. But in societies that have become highly integrated, not simply those in bondage, but others also, are tied to their localities. Of the ancient Mexicans, Zurita says: "The Indians never changed their village nor even their quarter. This custom was observed as a law." In ancient Peru, "it was not lawful for anyone to remove from one province, or village, to another"; and "any who traveled without just cause were punished as vagabonds." Elsewhere, along with that development of the militant type accompanying aggregation, there have been imposed restraints on movement under other forms. In ancient Egypt there existed a system of registration, and all citizens had periodically to report themseves to local officers. "Every Japanese is registered, and, whenever he removes his residence, the Nanushi, or head-man of the temple, gives a certificate." And then, in despotically governed European countries, we have more or less rigorous passport-systems, hindering the movements of citizens from place to place, and in some cases preventing them from leaving the country.

In these, as in other respects, however, the restraints which the social aggregate exercises over its units decrease as the industrial type begins greatly to qualify the militant type; partly because the societies characterized by industrialism are amply populous, and have superfluous members to fill the places of those who leave them, and partly because, in the absence of the oppressions accompanying a militant *régime,* a sufficient cohesion results from pecuniary interests, family bonds, and love of country.

Thus, saying nothing for the present of that political evolution manifested by increase of structure, and restricting ourselves to that political evolution manifested by increase of mass, here distinguished as political integration, we find that this has the following traits:

While the aggregates are small, the incorporation of materials for growth is carried on at one another's expense in feeble ways—by taking one another's game, by robbing one another of women, and, occasionally, by adopting one another's men. As larger aggregates are formed, incorporations proceed in more wholesale ways: first, by enslaving the separate members of conquered tribes, and presently by the bodily annexation of such tribes. And, as compound aggregates pass into doubly and trebly compound ones, there arise increasing desires to absorb adjacent smaller societies, and so to form still larger aggregates.

Conditions of several kinds further or hinder social growth and consolidation. The habitat may be fitted or unfitted for supporting a large population; or it may, by great or small facilities for intercourse within its area, favor or impede coöperation; or it may, by presence or absence of natural barriers, make easy or difficult the keeping together of the individuals under that coercion which is at first needful. And, as the antecedents of the race determine, the individuals may have in greater or less degrees the physical, the emotional, and the intellectual natures fitting them for combined action.

While the extent to which social integration can in each case be carried depends in part on these conditions, it also depends in part upon the degree of likeness among the units. At first, while the nature is so little molded to social life that cohesion is small, aggregation is largely dependent on ties of blood, implying great degrees of likeness. Groups in which such ties, and the resulting congruity, are most marked, and which, having family traditions in common, a common male ancestor, and a joint worship of him, are in these further ways made alike in ideas and sentiments, are groups in which the greatest social cohesion and power of cooperation arise. For a long time the clans and tribes descending from such primitive patriarchal groups have their political concert facilitated by this bond of relationship and the likeness it involves. Only after adaptation to social life has made considerable progress does harmonious cooperation among those who are not of the same stock become practicable; and even then their unlikenesses of nature must fall within moderate limits. Where the unlikenesses of nature are great, the society, held together only by force, tends to disintegrate when the force fails.

Likeness in the units forming a social group being one condition of their integration, a further condition is their joint reaction against external action; cooperation in war is the active cause of social integration. The temporary unions of savages for offense and defense show us the initiatory step.

When many tribes unite against a common enemy, long continuance of their combined action makes them coherent under some common control. And so it is subsequently with still larger aggregates.

Progress in social integration is both a cause and a consequence of a decreasing separableness among the units. Primitive wandering hordes exercise no such restraints over their members as prevent them individually from leaving one horde and joining another at will. Where tribes are more developed, desertion of one and admission into another are less easy—the assemblages are not so loose in composition. And, throughout those long stages during which societies are being enlarged and consolidated by militancy, the mobility of the units is more and more restrained. Only with that substitution of voluntary cooperation for compulsory cooperation which characterizes developing industrialism do these restraints disappear: enforced union being in such societies adequately replaced by spontaneous union.

A remaining truth to be named is that political integration, as it advances, tends to obliterate the original divisions among the united parts. In the first place, there is the slow disappearance of those nontopographical divisions arising from relationship, and resulting in separate gentes and tribes, gentile and tribal divisions, which are for a long time maintained after larger societies have been formed: gradual intermingling destroys them. In the second place, the smaller local societies united into a larger one, which at first retain their separate organizations, lose them by long cooperation: a common organization begins to ramify through them, and their individualities become indistinct. And, in the third place, there simultaneously results a more or less decided obliteration of their topographical bounds, and a replacing of these by the new administrative bound of the common organization. Hence naturally results the converse truth that, in the course of social dissolution, the great groups separate first, and afterward, if dissolution continues, these separate into their component smaller groups. Instance the ancient empires successively

58

formed in the East, the united kingdoms of which severally resumed their autonomies when the coercion keeping them together ceased. Instance, again, the Carlovingian empire, which, first parting into its large divisions, became in course of time further disintegrated by subdivision of these. And where, as in this last case, the process of dissolution goes very far, there is a return to something like the primitive condition, under which small predatory societies are engaged in continuous warfare with like small societies around them.

IV. Political Differentiation

The general law, that like units exposed to like forces tend to integrate, was in the last chapter exemplified by the formation of social groups. The clustering of men who are similar in kind, when similarly subject to hostile actions from without, and similarly reacting against them, we saw to be the first step in social evolution. Here the correlative general law, that in proportion as the like units of an aggregate are exposed to unlike forces they tend to form differentiated parts of the aggregate, has to be observed in its application to such groups, as the second step in social evolution.

The primary political differentiation originates from the primary family differentiation. Men and women being, by the unlikenesses of their functions in life, exposed to tinlike influences, begin from the first to assume unlike positions in the social group as they do in the family group: very early they respectively form the two political classes of rulers and ruled. And, how truly such dissimilarity of social positions as arises between them is caused by dissimilarity in their relations to surrounding actions, we shall see, on observing that the one is small or great according as the other is small or great. When treating of the *status* of women, it was pointed out that to a considerable degree among the Chippewas, and to a still greater degree among the Clatsops and Chinooks, "who live upon fish and roots, which the women are equally expert with the men in procuring, the former have a rank and influence very rarely found among Indians." We saw also that in Cueba, where the women join the men in war, "fighting by their side," their position is much higher than usual among rude peoples; and, similarly, that in Dahomey, where the women are as much warriors as the men, they are so regarded that, in the political organization, "the woman is officially superior," On contrasting these exceptional cases with the ordinary cases, in which the men, solely occupied in war and the chase, have unlimited authority, while the women, occupied in gathering miscellaneous small food and carrying burdens, are abject slaves, it becomes manifest that diversity of relations to surrounding actions initiates diversity of social positions. And, as we before saw, this truth is further illustrated by those few uncivilized societies which are habitually peaceful, such as the Bodo and Dhimáls of the Indian hills, and the ancient Pueblos of North America—societies in which the occupations are not, or were not broadly divided into fighting and working, and severally assigned to the two sexes; and in which, along with a comparatively small difference in the activities of the sexes, there goes, or went, small difference of social *status.*

So is it when we pass from the greater or less political differentiation which accompanies difference of sex to that which is independent of sex—to that which arises among men. Where the life is permanently peaceful, definite class-divisions do not exist. One of the Indian Hill-tribes, to which I have frequently referred as exhibiting the honesty, truthfulness, and amiability accompanying a purely industrial life, may be instanced. Hodgson says, "All Bodo and all Dhimáls are equal—absolutely so in right or law—wonderfully so in fact." The like is said of another peaceful and amiable Hill-tribe: "The Lepchas have no caste distinctions." And among a different race, the Papuans, may be named the peaceful Arafuras as displaying a "brotherly love with one another," and as having no divisions of rank.

As, at first, the domestic relation between the sexes passes into a political relation, such that men and women become, in militant groups, the ruling class and the subject class, so does the relation between master and slave, originally a domestic one, pass into a political one as fast as, by habitual war, the making of slaves becomes general. It is with the formation of a slave-class that there begins that political differentiation between the regulating structures and the sustaining structures which continues throughout all higher forms of social evolution.

61

Kane remarks that "slavery in its most cruel form exists among the Indians of the whole coast from California to Behring's Straits, the stronger tribes making slaves of all the others they can conquer. In the interior, where there is but little warfare, slavery does not exist." And this statement does but exhibit, in a distinct form, the truth everywhere obvious. Evidence suggests that the practice of enslavement diverged by small steps from the practice of cannibalism. Concerning the Nootkas, we read that "slaves are occasionally sacrificed and feasted upon"; and if we contrast this usage with the usage common elsewhere, of slaying and devouring captives as soon as they are taken, we may infer that the keeping of captives too numerous to be immediately eaten, with the view of eating them subsequently, leading, as it would, to the employment of them in the mean time, led to the discovery that their services might be of more value than their flesh, and so initiated the habit of preserving them as slaves. Be this as it may, however, we find that very generally, among tribes to which habitual militancy has given some slight degree of the appropriate structure, the enslavement of prisoners becomes an established habit. That women and children taken in war, and such men as have not been slain, naturally fall into unqualified servitude is manifest. They belong absolutely to their captors, who might have killed them, and who retain the right afterward to kill them, if they please. They become property, of which any use whatever may be made.

The acquirement of slaves, which is at first an incident of war, becomes presently an object of war. Of the Nootkas we read that "some of the smaller tribes at the north of the island are practically regarded as slave-breeding tribes, and are attacked periodically by stronger tribes"; and the like happens among the Chinooks. It was thus in ancient Vera Paz, where periodically they made "an inroad into the enemy's territory, . . . and captured as many as they wanted"; and it was so in Honduras, where, in declaring war, they gave their enemies notice that "they wanted slaves." Similarly with various existing peoples. St. John says that "many of the Dyaks are more desirous to obtain slaves than heads, and in attacking a village kill only those who resist or attempt to escape." And that in Africa slave-making wars are common needs no proof.

The class-division, thus initiated by war, afterward maintains and strengthens itself in sundry ways. Very soon there begins the custom of purchase. The Chinooks, besides slaves who have been captured, have slaves who were bought as children from their neighbors; and, as we saw when dealing with the domestic relations, the selling of their children into slavery is by no means uncommon with savages. Then the slave-class, thus early enlarged by purchase, comes afterward to be otherwise enlarged. There is voluntary acceptance of slavery for the sake of protection; there is enslavement for debt; there is enslavement for crime.

Leaving details, we need here note only that this political differentiation which war begins is effected, not by the bodily incorporation of other societies, or whole classes belonging to other societies, but by the incorporation of single members of other societies, and by like individual accretions. Composed of units who are detached from their original social relations and from one another, and absolutely attached to their owners, the slave-class is, at first, but indistinctly separated as a social stratum. It acquires separateness only as fast as there arise some restrictions on the powers of the owners. Ceasing to stand in the position of domestic cattle, slaves begin to form a division of the body-politic, when their personal claims begin to be distinguished as limiting the claims of their masters.

It is commonly supposed that serfdom arises by mitigation of slavery; but examination of the facts shows that it arises in a different way. While, during the early struggles for existence between them, primitive tribes, growing at one another's expense by incorporating separately the individuals they capture, thus form a class of absolute slaves, the formation of a servile class, considerably higher, and having a distinct social *status,* accompanies that later and larger process of growth under which one society incorporates other societies bodily. Serfdom originates along with conquest and annexation.

For whereas the one implies that the captured people are detached from their homes, the other implies that the subjugated people continue in their homes. Thomson remarks that, "among the New-Zealanders, whole tribes sometimes became nominally slaves when conquered, although permitted to live at their usual places of residence, on condition of paying tribute, in food, etc."—a statement which shows the origin of kindred arrangements in allied societies. Of the Sandwich Islands government when first known, described as consisting of a king with turbulent chiefs, who had been subjected in comparatively recent times, Ellis writes, "The common people are generally considered as attached to the soil, and are transferred with the land from one chief to another." Before the late changes in Feejee, there were enslaved districts; and of their inhabitants we read that they had to supply the chiefs' houses "with daily food, and build and keep them in repair." Though conquered peoples, thus placed, differ widely in the degrees of their subjection being at the one extreme, as in Feejee, liable to be eaten when wanted, and at the other extreme called on only to give specified proportions of produce or labor yet they remain alike as being undetached from their original places of residence. That serfdom in Europe originated in an analogous way there is good reason to believe. In Greece we have the case of Crete, where, under the conquering Dorians, there existed a vassal population, formed, it would seem, partly of the aborigines and partly of preceding conquerors, of which the first were serfs attached to lands of the state and of individuals, and the others had become tributary land-owners. In Sparta the like relations were established by like causes: there were the helots, who lived on, and cultivated, the lands of their Spartan masters, and the periæci, who had probably been, before the Dorian invasion, the superior class. So was it also in the Greek colonies afterward founded, such as Syracuse, where the aborigines became serfs. Similarly in later times and nearer regions. When Gaul was overrun by the Romans, and again when Romanized Gaul was overrun by the Franks, there was

64

little displacement of the actual cultivators of the soil, but these simply fell into lower positions: certainly lower political positions, and M. Guizot thinks lower industrial positions. Our own country, too, furnishes good illustrations. In ancient British times, writes Pearson, "it is probable that, in parts at least, there were servile villages, occupied by a kindred but conquered race, the first occupants of the soil." More trustworthy, but to the like effect, is the evidence which comes to us from old English days and Norman days. Professor Stubbs says: "The ceorl had his right in the common land of his township; his Latin name, villanus, had been a symbol of freedom, but his privileges were bound to the land, and when the Norman lord took the land he took the villein with it. Still the villein retained his customary rights, his house and land and rights of wood and hay; his lord's demesne depended for cultivation on his services, and he had in his lord's sense of self-interest the sort of protection that was shared by the horse and the ox." And of kindred import is the following passage from Innes: "I have said that, of the inhabitants of the Grange, the lowest in the scale was the *ceorl, bond, serf,* or villein, who was transferred like the land on which he labored, and who might be caught and brought back if he attempted to escape, like a stray ox or sheep. Their legal name of *nativus,* or *neyf,* which I have not found but in Britain, seems to point to their origin in the native race, the original possessors of the soil. . . . In the register of Dunfermline are numerous 'genealogies,' or stud-books, for enabling the lord to trace and reclaim his stock of serfs by descent. It is observable that most of them are of Celtic names."

Clearly, a subjugated territory, useless without cultivators, was left in the hands of the original cultivators because nothing was to be gained by putting others in their places, even could an adequate number of others be had. Hence, while it became the conqueror's interest to tie each original cultivator to the soil, it also became his interest to let him have such an amount of produce as to maintain him and enable him to rear offspring, and also to protect him against injuries which would incapacitate him for work.

To show how fundamental is the distinction between bondage of the primitive type and the bondage of serfdom, it needs but to add that, while the one can and does exist among savages and pastoral tribes, the other becomes possible only after the agricultural stage is reached; for only then can there occur the bodily annexation of one society by another, and only then can there be any tying to the soil.

Associated men, who live by hunting, and to whom the area occupied is of value only as a habitat for game, cannot well have anything more than a common participation in the use of this occupied area: such ownership of it as they have must be joint ownership. Naturally, then, at the outset, all the adult males, who are at once hunters and warriors, are the common possessors of the undivided land, encroachment on which by other tribes they resist. Though, in the earlier pastoral state, especially where the barrenness of the region involves wide dispersion, there is no definite proprietorship of the tract wandered over; yet, as is shown us in the strife between-the herdsmen of Abraham and those of Lot respecting feeding-grounds, some claims to exclusive use tend to arise; and at a later half-pastoral stage, as among the ancient Germans, the wanderings of each division fall within prescribed limits. I refer to these facts by way of showing the identity established at the outset between the militant class and the land-owning class. For, whether the group is one which lives by hunting or one which lives by feeding cattle, any slaves its members possess are excluded from land-ownership—the freemen, who are all fighting men, become, as a matter of course, the proprietors of their territory. This connection, in variously modified forms, long continues through subsequent stages of social evolution, and could scarcely do otherwise. Land being, in early settled communities, the almost exclusive source of wealth, it happens inevitably that, during times in which the principle that might is right remains unqualified, personal power and possession of land go together. Hence the fact that, where, instead of being held by the whole society, land comes to be parceled out among component village communities, or among families, or among individuals, possession of it habitually goes along with the bearing of arms. In ancient Egypt "every soldier was a land-owner"—"had an allotment of land of about six acres." In Greece the invading Hellenes, wresting the soil from its original holders, joined military service with the land-ownership. In Rome, too, "every freeholder, from the seventeenth to the sixtieth year of his age, was under obligation of service, . . . so that even the emancipated slave had to serve, who, in an exceptional case, bad come into possession of landed property." The like happened in the early Teutonic community. Joined with professional warriors, its army included "the mass of freemen, arranged in families, fighting for their homesteads and hearths": such freemen, or markmen, owning land partly in common and partly as individual proprietors. Similarly with the ancient English: "Their occupation of the land as *cognationes* resulted from their enrollment in the field, where each kindred was drawn up under an officer of its own lineage and appointment"; and so close was this dependence that "a thane forfeited his hereditary freehold by misconduct in battle."

Beyond the original connection between militancy and land-owning, which naturally arises from the joint interest which those who own the land and occupy it, either individually or collectively, have in resisting aggressors, there arises later a further connection. As, along with successful militancy, there progresses a social evolution which gives to a dominant ruler increased power, it becomes his custom to reward his leading soldiers by grants of land. Early Egyptian kings "bestowed on distinguished military officers" portions of the crown domains. When the barbarians were enrolled as Roman soldiers, "they were paid also by assignments of land according to a custom which prevailed in the imperial armies. The possession of these lands was given to them on condition of the son becoming a soldier like his father." And that kindred usages were general throughout the feudal period is a familiar truth: feudal tenancy being, indeed, thus constituted, and inability to bear arms being a reason for excluding women from succession. To exemplify the nature of the relation established, it will suffice to name the facts that "William the Conqueror. . . distributed this kingdom into about sixty thousand parcels, of nearly equal value, from each of which the service of a soldier was due," and that one of his laws requires all owners of land to "swear that they become vassals or tenants," and will "defend their lord's territories and title as well as his person" by "knight service on horseback."

That this original relation between land-owning and militancy long survived, we are shown by the armorial bearings of county families, as well as by their portraits of ancestors who are mostly represented in military costume.

Setting out with the class of warriors, or men bearing arms, who in primitive communities are owners of the land, collectively or individually, or partly one and partly the other, there arises the question, How does this class differentiate into nobles and freemen?

The most general reply is, of course, that since the state of homogeneity is by necessity unstable, time inevitably brings about inequality of positions among those whose positions were at first equal. Before the semi-civilized state is reached the differentiation can not become decided, because there can be no large accumulations of wealth, and because the laws of descent do not favor maintenance of such accumulations as are possible. But in the pastoral and still more in the agricultural community, especially where descent through males has been established, several causes of differentiation come into play. There is first that of unlikeness of kinship to the head-man. Obviously, in course of generations, the younger descendants of the younger become more and more remotely related to the eldest descendant of the eldest, and social inferiority arises: as the obligation to execute blood-revenge for a murdered member of the family does not extend beyond a certain degree of relationship (in ancient France not beyond the seventh), so neither does the accompanying distinction. From the same cause comes inferiority in point of possessions. Inheritance by the eldest male from generation to generation brings about the result that those who are the most distantly connected in blood with the head of the group are also the poorest. And then there cooperates with these factors a consequent factor—namely, the extra power which the greater, wealth gives. For when there arise disputes within the tribe, the richer are those who, by their better appliances for defense and their greater ability to purchase aid, naturally have the advantage over the poorer. Proof that this is a potent cause is found in a fact named by Sir Henry Maine: "The founders of a part of our modern European aristocracy, the Danish, are known to have been originally peasants who fortified their houses during deadly village struggles, and then used their advantage." Such superiorities of power and position once initiated are increased in another way. Already in the last chapter we have seen that communities are to a certain extent increased by the addition of fugitives from other communities—sometimes criminals, sometimes those who are oppressed. While, in places where such fugitives belong to races of superior type, they often become rulers (as among many Indian Hill-tribes, whose rajahs are of Hindoo extraction), in places where they are of the same race, and can not do this, they attach themselves to those of chief power in their adopted tribe. Sometimes they yield up their freedom for the sake of protection: a man will make himself a slave by breaking a spear in the presence of his wished-for master, as among the East Africans, or by inflicting some small bodily injury upon him, as among the Fulahs. And in ancient Rome the semi-slave class distinguished as clients originated by this voluntary acceptance of servitude with safety. But, where his aid promises to be of value as a warrior, the fugitive offers himself in that capacity in exchange for maintenance and refuge. Other things equal, he joins himself to someone marked by superiority of power and property, and thus enables the man already dominant to become more dominant. Such armed dependents, having as aliens no claims to the lands of the group, and bound to its head only by fealty, answer in position to the *comites* as found in the early German communities, and as exemplified in old English times by the "Huscarlas" (house-carls), with whom nobles surrounded themselves. Evidently, too, followers of this kind, having certain interests in common with their protector, and no interests in common with the rest of the community, become, in his hands, the means of usurping communal rights and elevating himself while depressing the rest.

Step by step the contrast strengthens. Beyond such as have voluntarily made themselves slaves to a head-man, others have become enslaved by capture in the wars meanwhile going on, others by staking themselves in gaming, others by purchase, others by crime, others by debt. And of necessity the possession of many slaves, habitually accompanying wealth and power, tends still further to increase that wealth and power, and to mark off still more the higher rank from the lower.

Certain concomitant influences generate differences of nature, physical and mental, between those members of a community who have attained superior positions, and those who have remained inferior. Unlikenesses of *status* once initiated lead to unlikenesses of life, which, by the constitutional changes they work, presently make the unlikenesses of *status* more difficult to alter.

First there comes difference of diet and its effects. In the habit, common among primitive tribes, of letting the women subsist on the leavings of the men, and in the accompanying habit of denying to the younger men certain choice viands which the older men eat, we see exemplified the inevitable proclivity of the strong to feed themselves at the expense of the weak; and, when there arise class-divisions, there habitually results better nutrition of the superior than of the inferior. Forster remarks that in the Society Islands the lower classes often suffer from a scarcity of food which never extends to the upper classes. In the Sandwich Islands the flesh of such animals as they have is eaten principally by the chiefs. Of cannibalism among the Feejeeans, Seeman says, "The common people throughout the group, as well as women of all classes, were by custom debarred from it." These instances sufficiently indicate the contrast that everywhere arises between the diets of the ruling few and of the subject many. And then by such differences of diet, and accompanying differences in clothing, shelter, and strain on the energies, are eventually produced physical differences. Of the Feejeeans we read that "the chiefs are tall, well made, and muscular; while the lower orders manifest the meagerness arising from laborious service and scanty nourishment." The chiefs among the Sandwich-Islanders "are tall and stout, and their personal appearance is so much superior to that of the common people that some have imagined them a distinct race." Ellis, verifying Cook, says of the Tahitians, that the chiefs are, "almost without exception, as much superior to the peasantry. . . in physical strength as they are in rank and circumstances"; and Erskine notes a parallel contrast among the Tongans. That the like holds among the African races may be inferred from Reade's remark that "the court lady is tall and elegant; her skin smooth and transparent; her beauty has stamina and longevity. The girl of the middle classes, so frequently pretty, is very often short and coarse, and soon becomes a matron; while, if you descend to the lower classes, you will find good looks rare, and the figure angular, stunted, sometimes almost deformed."

Simultaneously there arise, between the ruling and subject classes, unlikenesses of bodily activity and skill. Occupied, as those of higher rank commonly are, in the chase when not occupied in war, they have a life-long discipline of a kind conducive to various physical superiorities; while, contrariwise, those occupied in agriculture, in carrying of burdens, and in other drudgeries, partially lose what agility and address they naturally had. Class-predominance is, therefore, thus further facilitated.

And then there are the respective mental traits produced by daily exercise of power, and by daily submission to power. The ideas, and sentiments, and modes of behavior, perpetually repeated, generate on one side an inherited fitness for command, and on the other side an inherited fitness for obedience; with the result that, in course of time, there arises on both sides the belief that the established relations of classes are the natural ones.

By implying habitual war among settled societies, the foregoing interpretations have implied the formation of compound societies. The rise of such class-divisions as have been described is, therefore, complicated by the rise of further class-divisions determined by the relations from time to time established between those conquerors and conquered whose respective groups already contain class-divisions.

This increasing differentiation which accompanies increasing integration is clearly seen in certain semi-civilized societies, such as that of the Sandwich-Islanders. Ellis enumerates their ranks as—"1. King, queens, and royal family, along with the councilor or chief minister of the king. 2. The governors of the different islands, and the chiefs of several large divisions. Many of these are descendants of those who were kings of the respective islands in Cook's time, and until subdued by Kamehameha. 3. Chiefs of districts or villages, who pay a regular rent for the land, cultivating it by means of their dependents, or letting it out to tenants. This rank includes also the ancient priests. 4. The laboring classes—those renting small portions of land, those working on the land for food and clothing, mechanics, musicians, and dancers." And, as shown by other passages, the laboring classes here grouped together are divisible into—artisans, who are paid wages; serfs, attached to the soil; and slaves. Inspection makes it tolerably clear that the lowest chiefs, once independent, were reduced to the second rank when adjacent chiefs conquered them and became local kings; and that they were reduced to the third rank at the same time that these local kings became chiefs of the second rank, when, by conquest, a kingship of the whole group was established. Other societies in kindred stages show us kindred divisions similarly to be accounted for. Among the New-Zealanders there are six grades; there are six among the

Ashantees; there are five among the Abyssinians; and other more or less compounded African states present analogous divisions. Perhaps ancient Peru furnishes as clear a case as any of the superposition of ranks resulting from subjugation. The petty kingdoms which were massed together by the conquering Incas were severally left with the rulers and their subordinates undisturbed; but over the whole empire there was a superior organization of Inca rulers of various grades. That kindred causes produced kindred effects in early Egyptian times is inferable from traditions and remains which tell us both of local struggles which ended in consolidation and of conquests by invading races; whence would naturally result the numerous divisions and subdivisions which Egyptian society presented: an inference justified by the fact that under Roman dominion there was a recomplication caused by superposing of Roman governing agencies upon native governing agencies. Passing over other ancient instances, and coming to the familiar case of our own country, we may note how, from the followers of the conquering Norman, there arose the two ranks of the greater and lesser barons, holding their land directly from the king, while the old English thanes were reduced to the rank of sub-feudatories. Of course, where perpetual wars produce, first, small aggregations, and then larger ones, and then dissolutions, and then reaggregations, and then unions of them, various in their extents, as happened in mediaeval Europe, there result very numerous divisions. In the Merovingian kingdoms there were slaves having seven different origins; there were serfs of more than one grade; there were freedmen—men who, though emancipated, did not rank with the fully free; and there were two other classes less than free—the *liten* and the *coloni*. Of the free there were three classes—independent land-owners; freemen in relations of dependence with other freemen, of whom there were two kinds; and freemen in special relations with the king, of whom there were three kinds.

And here, while observing in these various cases how greater political differentiation is made possible by greater political integration, we may also observe that in early stages, while social cohesion is small, greater political integration is made possible by greater political differentiation. For the larger the mass to be held together, while incoherent, the more numerous must be the agents standing in successive degrees of subordination to hold it together.

The political differentiations which militancy originates, and which for a long time acquire increasing definiteness, so that intermixture of ranks by marriage is made a crime, are at later stages and under other conditions interfered with, traversed, and partially or wholly destroyed.

Where, throughout long periods and in ever-varying degrees, war has been producing aggregations and dissolutions, the continual breaking up and reforming of social bonds obscures the original divisions established in the ways described: instance the state of things in the Merovingian kingdoms just named. And where, instead of conquests by kindred adjacent societies, which in large measure leave standing the social positions and properties of the subjugated, there are conquests by alien races carried on more barbarously, the original grades may be practically obliterated, and in place of them there may arise grades originating entirely by appointment of the despotic conqueror. In parts of the East, where such overrunnings of race by race have been going on from the earliest recorded times, we see this state of things substantially realized: there is little or nothing of hereditaryrank, and the only rank recognized is that of official position. Besides the different grades of appointed state functionaries, there are no class distinctions, or none having political meanings.

A tendency to subordination of the original ranks and a substitution of new ranks is otherwise caused: it accompanies the progress of political consolidation. The change which has occurred in China well illustrates this effect. Gutzlaff says: "Mere title was afterward (on the decay of the feudal system) the reward bestowed by the sovereign, . . . and the haughty and powerful grandees of other countries are here the dependent and penurious servants of the Crown, ., . The revolutionary principle of leveling all classes has been carried in China to a very great extent. . . . This is introduced for the benefit of the sovereign, to render his authority supreme."

The causes of such changes are not difficult to see. In the first place, the subjugated local rulers losing, as integration advances, more and more of their power, lose, consequently, more and more of their actual if not of their nominal rank, passing from the condition of tributary rulers to the condition of subjects. Indeed, jealousy on the part of the monarch sometimes prompts positive exclusion of them from influential positions; as in France, where "Louis XIV systematically excluded the nobility from ministerial functions." Presently their distinction is further diminished by the rise of competing ranks created by state authority. Instead of the titles inherited by the landpossessing military chiefs, which were descriptive of their attributes and positions, there come to be titles conferred by the sovereign. Certain of the classes thus established are still of militant origin; as the knights made on the battle-field, sometimes in large numbers before battle, as at Agincourt, when five hundred were thus created, and sometimes afterward in reward for valor. Others of them arise from the exercise of political functions of different grades; as in France, where, in the seventeenth century, hereditary nobility was conferred on officers of the great council and officers of the chamber of accounts—officers who had habitually been of *bourgeois* extraction. The administration of law, too, presently originates titles of honor. In France, in 1607, nobility was granted to doctors, regents, and professors of law; and "the superior courts obtained, in 1644, the privileges of nobility of the first degree." "So that," as Warnkoenig remarks, "the original conception of nobility was in the course of time so much widened that its primitive relation to the possession of a fief is no longer recognizable, and the whole institution seems changed." These, with kindred instances, which our own country and other European countries furnish, show us both how the original class-divisions become blurred and how the new class-divisions are distinguished by being delocalized. They are strata which run through the integrated society, having, many of them, no reference to the land, and no more connection with one place than another. It is true that, of the titles artificially conferred, the higher are habitually derived from the names of districts and towns: so simulating, but only simulating, the ancient feudal titles expressive of actual lordship over territories. The other modern titles, however, which have arisen with the growth of political, judicial, and other functions, have not even nominal references to localities. This change naturally accompanies the growing integration of the parts into a whole, and the rise of an organization of the whole which disregards the divisions among the parts.

More effective still, in weakening those primitive political divisions initiated by militancy, is increasing industrialism. This acts in two ways, firstly, by creating a class having power derived otherwise than from territorial possessions or official position; and, secondly, by generating ideas and sentiments at variance with the ancient assumptions of class-superiority. As we have already seen, rank and wealth are at the outset habitually associated. Existing uncivilized people still show us this relation. The chief of a kraal among the Koranna Hottentots is "usually the person of greatest property." In the Bechuana language "the word *kosi. . .* has a double acceptation, denoting either a chief or a rich man." Such small authority as a Chinook chief has, "rests on riches, which consists in wives, children, slaves, boats, and shells." So was it originally in Europe. In ancient Spain the title *ricos hombres,* applied to the barons, definitely identified the two attributes. Indeed, it is manifest that before the development of commerce, and while possession of land could alone give largeness of means, lordship and riches were directly connected; so that, as Sir Henry Maine remarks, "the opposition commonly set up between birth and wealth, and particularly wealth other than landed property, is entirely modern." When, however, with the arrival of industry at that stage in which wholesale transactions bring large profits, there arise traders who vie with, and exceed, many of the landed nobility in wealth, and when, by conferring obligations on kings and nobles, such traders gain social influence, there comes an occasional removal of the barrier between them and the titled classes. In France the progress began as early as 1271, when there were issued letters ennobling Raoul, the goldsmith—"the first letters conferring nobility in existence." The precedent, once established, is followed with increasing frequency, and sometimes, under pressure of financial needs, there grows up the practice of selling titles, in disguised ways or openly. In France, in 1702, the king ennobled two hundred persons at three thousand livres a head; in 1706, five hundred at six thousand a head. And then, the breaking down of the ancient political divisions thus caused, is furthered by that weakening of them consequent on the growing spirit of equality fostered by industrial life. In proportion as men are daily habituated to maintain their own claims while respecting the claims of others, which they do in every act of exchange, whether of goods for money or of services for pay, there is produced a mental attitude at variance with that which accompanies subjection; and, as fast as this happens, such political distinctions as imply subjection lose more and more of that respect which gives them strength.

Class-distinctions, then, date back to the beginnings of social life. Omitting those small wandering assemblages which are so incoherent that their component parts are ever changing their relations to one another and to the environment we see that, wherever there is some coherence and some permanence of relation among the parts, there begin to arise political divisions. Relative superiority of power, first causing a differentiation at once domestic and social, between the activities and positions of the sexes, presently begins to cause a differentiation among males, shown in the bondage of captives; a master-class and a slave-class are formed.

Where men continue the wandering life in pursuit of wild food for themselves or their cattle, the groups they form are debarred from doing more by war than appropriate one another's units individually; but, where men have passed into the agricultural or settled state, it becomes possible for one community to take possession bodily of another community, along with the territory it occupies. When this happens, there arise additional class-divisions. The conquered and tribute-paying community, besides having its head-men reduced to subjection, has its people reduced to a state such that, while they continue to live on their lands, they yield up, through the intermediation of their chiefs, part of the produce to the conquerors; so foreshadowing what eventually becomes a serf-class.

From the beginning the militant class, being by force of arms the dominant class, becomes the class which owns the source of food—the land. During the hunting and pastoral stages, the warriors of the group hold the land collectively. On passing into the settled state, their tenures become partly collective and partly individual in sundry ways, and eventually almost wholly individual. But, throughout long stages of social evolution, land-owning and militancy continue to be associated.

The class-differentiation, of which militancy is the active cause, is furthered by the establishment of definite descent, and especially male descent, and the transmission of position and property to the eldest son of the eldest continually. This conduces to inequalities of position and wealth between near kindred and remote kindred; and such inequalities of wealth, once initiated, strengthen themselves by giving to the superior increased means of maintaining their power by accumulating appliances for offense and defense.

Such differentiation is increased, at the same time that a new differentiation is initiated, by the immigration of fugitives who attach themselves to the most powerful member of the group, now as dependents who work, and now as armed followers—armed followers who form a class bound to the dominant man, and unconnected with the land. And since, in clusters of such groups, fugitives ordinarily flock most to the strongest group, and become adherents of its head, they are instrumental in furthering those subsequent integrations and differentiations which conquests bring about.

Inequalities of social position, bringing inequalities in the supplies and kinds of food, clothing, and shelter, tend to establish physical differences, to the further advantage of the rulers and disadvantage of the ruled. And, beyond the physical differences, there are produced, by the respective habits of life, mental differences, emotional and intellectual, strengthening the general contrast of nature.

When there come the conquests which produce compound societies, and, again, doubly compound ones, there come superpositions of ranks. And the general effect is that, while the ranks of the conquering society become respectively higher than those which existed before, those of the conquered become respectively lower.

The class-divisions thus formed during the earlier stages of militancy are traversed and obscured as fast as the many small societies are consolidated into one large society. Ranks referring to local organization are gradually replaced by ranks referring to general organization. Instead of deputy and sub-deputy governing agents who are the militant owners of the subdivisions they rule, there come governing agents who more or less clearly form strata running throughout the society as a whole—a concomitant of developed political administration.

Chiefly, however, we have to note that, while the higher political evolution of large social aggregates tends to break down the divisions of rank which grew up in the small component social aggregate, by substituting other divisions, these original divisions are still more broken down by growing industrialism. Generating a wealth that is not connected with rank, this initiates a competing power; and at the same time, by establishing the equal positions of citizens before the law in respect of trading transactions, it weakens those divisions which at the outset expressed inequalities of position before the law.

As verifying these interpretations, I may add that they harmonize with the interpretations of ceremonial institutions recently given. As the primary differences of rank result from victories, and as the primary forms of propitiation originate in the behavior of the vanquished to the vanquishers, so the later differences of rank result from differences of power which, in the last resort, express themselves in physical coercion, and so the observances between ranks are recognitions of such differences of power. When the conquered enemy is made a slave, and mutilated by taking a trophy from his body, we see simultaneously originating the deepest political distinction and the ceremony which marks it; and, with the continued militancy that compounds and recompounds social groups, there goes at once the development of political distinctions and the development of ceremonies marking them. And, as we before saw that growing industrialism diminishes the rigor of ceremonial rule, so here we see that it tends to destroy those class-divisions which militancy originates, and to establish others which indicate differences of position consequent on differences of aptitude for the various functions which an industrial society needs.

V. Political Forms and Forces

The conceptions of biologists have been greatly advanced by the discovery that organisms which, when adult, appear to have scarcely anything in common, were, in their first stages, very similar; and that, indeed, all organisms start with a common structure. Recognition of this truth has revolutionized not only their ideas respecting the relations of organisms to one another, but also respecting the relations of the parts of each organism to one another.

If societies have evolved, and if that mutual dependence of their parts which social cooperation implies, and which constitutes them organized bodies, has been gradually reached, then the implication is that, however unlike their developed structures become, there is a rudimentary structure with which they all set out. And, if there can be recognized any such primitive unity, recognition of it will help us to interpret the ultimate diversity. We shall understand better how in each society the several components of the political agency have come to be what we now see them, and how those of one society are related to those of another.

Setting out with an unorganized horde, including both sexes and all ages, let us ask what must happen when some question, as that of migration or defense against enemies, has to be decided. The assembled individuals will fall, more or less clearly, into two divisions. The elder, the stronger, and those whose sagacity and courage have been proved by experience, will form the smaller part, who carry on the discussion, while the larger part, formed of the young, the weak, and the undistinguished, will be listeners, who usually go no further than to express from time to time assent or dissent. A further inference may safely be drawn. In the cluster of leading men there is sure to be someone whose weight is greater than that of any other—some aged hunter, some distinguished warrior, some cunning medicine man, who will have more than his individual share in forming the resolution finally acted upon. That is to say, the entire assemblage will resolve itself into three parts. To use a biological metaphor, there will, out of the general mass, be differentiated a nucleus and a nucleolus.

These first traces of political structure, which we infer *a priori* must spontaneously arise, we find have arisen among the rudest peoples; repetition having so strengthened them as to produce a settled order. When, among the aborigines of Victoria, a tribe plans revenge on another tribe supposed to have killed one of its members, "a council is called of all the old men of the tribe. . . . The women form an outer circle round the men. . . . The chief [simply 'a native of influence'] opens the council," And what we here see happening in an assemblage having no greater differences than those based on strength, age, and capacity, happens when, later, these natural distinctions have gained definiteness. In illustration may be named the account which Schoolcraft gives of a conference at which the Chippewas, Ottawas, and Pottawattamies, met certain United States commissioners, Schoolcraft being himself present. After the address of the head commissioner had been delivered, the speaking on behalf of the Indians was carried on by the principal chiefs; the lead being taken by "a man venerable for his age and standing." Though Schoolcraft does not describe the assemblage of undistinguished people, yet that they were present is shown by a passage in one of the native speeches: "Behold! see my brethren, both young and old—the warriors and chiefs—the women and children of my nation." And that the political order observed on this occasion was the usual order, is implied by its recurrence even in parts of America where chiefs have become marked off by ascribed nobility; as instance the account quoted by Bancroft of one of the Central American tribes, who "have frequent reunions in their council-house at night. The hall is then lighted up by a large fire, and the people sit with uncovered heads, listening respectfully to the observations and decisions of the *ahuales*— men over forty years of age, who have occupied public positions, or distinguished themselves in some way." Among peoples unlike in type and remote in locality, we find, modified in detail but similar in general character, this primitive governmental form. Of the Hill tribes of India may be instanced the Khonds, of whom we read that "assemblies of the whole tribe, or of any of its subdivisions, are convened, to determine questions of general importance. The members of every society, however, have a right to be present at *all* its councils, and to give their voices on the questions mooted, although the patriarchs alone take a part in their public *discussion.* . . . The federal patriarchs, in like manner, consult with the heads of tribes, and assemble when necessary the entire population of the federal group."

In New Zealand the government was conducted in accordance with public opinion expressed in general assemblies; and the chiefs "could not declare peace or war, or do anything affecting the whole people, without the sanction of the majority of the clan." Of the Tahitians, Ellis tells us that the king had a few chiefs as advisers, but that no affair of national importance could be undertaken without consulting the land-holders or second rank, and also that public assemblies were held. Similarly of the Malagasy: "The greatest national council in Madagascar is an assembly of the people of the capital, and the heads of the provinces, towns, villages, etc." The king usually presides in person.

Though in these last cases we see considerable changes in the relative powers of the three components, so that the inner few have gained in authority at the expense of the outer many, yet all three are still present; and they continue to be present when we pass to sundry historic peoples. Even of the Phœnicians, Movers notes that "in the time of Alexander a war was decided upon by the Tyrians without the consent of the absent king, the senate acting together with the popular assembly." Then there is the familiar case of the Homeric Greeks, whose Agora, presided over by the king, was "an assembly for talk, communication and discussion to a certain extent by the chiefs, in presence of the people as listeners and sympathizers," who were seated around; and. that the people were not always passive is shown by the story of Thersites, who, ill-used though he was by Odysseus and derided by the crowd for interfering, had first made his harangue. Again, the king, the senate, and the freemen, in primitive Rome, stood in relations which had manifestly grown out of those existing in the original assembly; for, though the three did not simultaneously cooperate, yet on important occasions the king communicated his proposals to the assembled burgesses, who expressed their approval or disapproval, and the clan-chiefs, forming the senate, though they did not debate in public, had yet such joint power that they could, on occasion, negative the decision of king and burgesses. Concerning the primitive Germans, Tacitus, as translated by Mr. Freeman, writes: "On smaller matters the chiefs debate, on greater matters all men; but so that those things whose final decision rests with the whole people are first handled by the chiefs. . . . The multitude sits armed in such order as it thinks good; silence is proclaimed by the priests, who have also the right of enforcing it. Presently the king or chief, according to the age of each, according to his birth, according to his glory in war or his eloquence, is listened to, speaking rather by the influence of persuasion than by the power of commanding. If their opinions give offense, they are thrust aside with a shout; if they are approved, the hearers clash their spears."

Similarly among the Scandinavians, as shown us in Iceland, where, besides the general Al-thing annually held, which it was "disreputable for a freeman not to attend," and at which "people of all classes in fact pitched their tents," there were local assemblies called Var-things "attended by all the freemen of the district, with a crowd of retainers .. . both for the discussion of public affairs and the administration of justice. . . . Within the circle [formed for administering justice] sat the judges, the people standing on the outside." In the account given by Mr. Freeman of the yearly meetings in the Swiss cantons of Uri and Appenzell, we may trace this primitive political form as still existing; for though the presence of the people at large is the fact principally pointed out, yet there is named, in the case of Uri, the body of magistrates or chosen chiefs who form the second element, as well as the head magistrate who is the first element. And that in ancient England there was a kindred constitution of the Wittenagemot, is indirectly proved; as witness the following passage from Freeman's "Growth of the English Constitution": "No ancient record gives us any clear or formal account of the constitution of that body. It is commonly spoken of in a vague way as a gathering of the wise, the noble, the great men. But, alongside of passages like these, we find other passages which speak of it in a way which implies a far more popular constitution. King Eadward is said to be chosen king by 'all folk.' Earl Godwine 'makes his speech before the king and aU the people of the land.'" And the implication, as Mr. Freeman points out, is that the share taken by the people in the proceedings was that of expressing by shouts their approval or disapproval.

This form of ruling agency is thus shown to be the fundamental form, by its presence at the outset of social life and by its continuance under various conditions. Not among peoples of superior types only, such as Aryans and some Semites, do we find it, but also among sundry Malayo-Polynesians, among the red men of North America, the Dravidian tribes of the Indian hills, the aborigines of Australia. In fact, as already implied, governmental organization could not possibly begin in any other way. On the one hand, no controlling force at first exists save that of the aggregate will as manifested in the assembled horde. On the other hand, leading parts in determining this aggregate will are inevitably taken by the few whose superiority is recognized. And of these predominant men some one is sure to be most predominant. That which we have to note as specially significant, is not that a free form of government is the primitive form; though this is an implication which may be dwelt upon. Nor are we chiefly concerned with the fact that at the very beginning there shows itself that separation of the superior few from the inferior many, which becomes marked in later stages; though this, too, is a fact which may be singled out and emphasized. Nor is attention to be mainly directed to the early appearance of a controlling head, having power greater than that of any other; though the evidence given may be cited to prove this. But here we have to note, particularly, the truth that at the very outset may be discerned the vague outlines of a triune political structure.

Of course, the ratios among the powers of these three components are in no two cases quite the same; and, as implied in sundry of the above examples, they everywhere undergo more or less change—change determined here by the emotional natures of the men composing the group, there by the physical circumstances as favoring or hindering independence, now by the activities as warlike or peaceful, and now by the exceptional characters of particular individuals.

Unusual sagacity, skill, or strength, habitually regarded by primitive men as supernatural, may give to some member of the tribe an influence which, transmitted to a successor supposed to inherit his supernatural character, may generate a chiefly authority subordinating both that of the other leading men and that of the mass. Or a division of labor, such that while some of the tribe remain exclusively warriors the rest are in a measure otherwise occupied, may give to the two superior components of the political agency an ability to override the third. Or the members of the third, keeping up habits which make coercion of them difficult or impossible, may maintain a general predominance over the other two. And then the relations of these three governing elements to the entire community may, and ordinarily do, undergo change by the formation of a passive class, excluded from their deliberations—a class at first composed of the women and afterward containing also the slaves or other dependents.

War, successfully carried on, not only establishes the passive or non-political class, but also, implying as it does subordination, changes more or less decidedly the relative powers of these three parts of the political agency. As, other things equal, groups in which there is little or no subordination are subjugated by groups in which subordination is greater, there is a tendency to the survival and spread of groups in which the controlling power of the dominant few becomes relatively great. In like manner, since success in war largely depends on that promptitude and consistency of action which singleness of will gives, there must, where warfare is chronic, be a tendency for members of the ruling group to become more and more obedient to its head: disappearance in the struggle for existence, among tribes otherwise equal, being ordinarily a consequence of inadequate obedience. And then it is also to be noted that the overrunnings of societies one by another, repeated and re-repeated as they often are, have the effect of obscuring and even obliterating the traces of the original political form.

While, however, recognizing the fact that during political evolution these three primitive components alter their proportions in various ways and degrees, to the extent that some of them become mere rudiments or wholly disappear, it will greatly alter our conception of political forms if we remember that they are all derived from this primitive form— that a despotism, an oligarchy, or a democracy, is to be regarded as a type of government in which one of the original components has greatly developed at the expense of the other two, and that the various mixed types are to be arranged according to the degrees in which one or other of the original components has the greater influence.

Is there any fundamental unity of political forces accompanying this fundamental unity of political forms? While losing sight of the common origin of political structures, have we not also become inadequately conscious of the common source of their powers? How prone we are to forget the ultimate, while thinking of the proximate, it may be worth while pausing a moment to observe.

One, who in a storm watches the breaking-up of a wreck or the tearing down of a sea-wall, is impressed by the immense energy of the waves. Of course, when it is pointed out that in the absence of wind no such results can be produced, he recognizes the truth that the sea is in itself powerless, and that the power enabling it to destroy vessels and piers is given by the currents of air which roughen its surface. If he stops short here, however, he fails to identify the force which works these striking changes. Intrinsically, the air is just as passive as the water is. There would be no winds were it not for the varying effects of the sun's heat on different parts of the earth's surface. Even when he has traced back thus far the energy which undermines cliffs and makes shingle, he has not reached its source; for in the absence of that continuous concentration of the solar mass, caused by the mutual gravitation of its parts, there would be no solar radiations.

The tendency here illustrated, which all have in some degree and most in a great degree, to associate power with the visible agency exercising it, rather than with its inconspicuous source, has, as above implied, a vitiating influence on conceptions at large, and among others on political ones. Though the habit, general in past times, of regarding the powers of governments as inherent, has been, by the growth of popular institutions, a good deal qualified; yet, even now, there is no clear apprehension of the fact that governments are not themselves powerful, but are the instrumentalities of a power. This power existed before governments arose; governments were themselves produced by it; and it ever continues to be that which, disguised more or less completely, works through them. Let us go back to the beginning.

The Greenlanders are entirely without political control; having nothing which represents it more nearly than the deference paid to the opinion of some old man, skilled in seal-catching and the signs of the weather. But a Greenlander who is aggrieved by another has his remedy in what is called a singing combat. He composes a satirical poem, and challenges his antagonist to a satirical duel in face of the tribe: "He who has the last word wins the trial." And then Crantz adds: "Nothing so effectually restrains a Greenlander from vice as the dread of public disgrace." Here we see operating, in its original unqualified way, that governing influence of public sentiment which precedes more special governing influences.

88

The dread of social reprobation is in some cases enforced by the dread of banishment. Among the otherwise unsubordinated Australians, they "punish each other for such offenses as theft, sometimes by expulsion from the camp." Of one of the Columbian tribes we read that "the Salish can hardly be said to have any regular form of government"; and then, further, we read that "criminals are sometimes punished by banishment from their tribe." Certain aborigines of the Indian hills, widely unlike these Columbians in type and in their modes of life, show us a similar relation between undeveloped political restraint and the restraint of aggregate feeling. Among the Bodo and Dhimáls, whose village heads are simply respected elders with no coercive power, those who offend against customs "are admonished, fined, or excommunicated, according to the degree of the offense." But the controlling influence of public sentiment, in groups which have little or no political organization, is best shown in the force with which it acts on those who are bound to avenge murders. Concerning the Australian aborigines, Sir George Grey writes: "The holiest duty a native is called on to perform is that of avenging the death of his nearest relation, for it is his peculiar duty to do so; until he has fulfilled this task, he is constantly taunted by the old women; his wives, if he is married, would soon quit him; if he is unmarried, not a single young woman would speak to him; his mother would constantly cry, and lament that she should ever have given birth to so degenerate a son; his father would treat him with contempt, and reproaches would constantly be sounded in his ear."

We have next to note that, for a long time after political control has made its appearance, it remains conspicuously subordinate to this control of general feeling; both because, while there is no developed political organization, the head-man has little ability to enforce his will, and because such ability as he has, if unduly exercised, causes desertion. From all parts of the world may be cited illustrations. In America, among the Snake Indians, "each individual is his own master, and the only control to which his conduct is subjected is the

89

advice of a chief supported by his influence over the opinions of the rest of the tribe." Of a Chinook chief we are told that "his ability to render service to his neighbors, and the popularity which follows it, is at once the foundation and the measure of his authority." If a Dakota "wishes to do mischief, the only way a chief can influence him is to give him something, or pay him to desist from his evil intentions. The chief has no authority to act for the tribe, and dare not do it." And among the Creeks, more advanced in political organization though they are, the authority of the elected chiefs "continues during good behavior. The disapproval of the body of the people is an effective bar to the exercise of their powers and functions." Turning to Asia, we read that the *bais* or chiefs of the Kirghiz "have little power over them for good or evil. In consideration of their age and blood, some deference to their opinions is shown, but nothing more." The Ostiaks "pay respect, in the fullest sense of the word, to their chief, if wise and valiant, but this homage is voluntary, and founded on personal regard." And of the Naga chiefs Butler says, "Their orders are obeyed so far only as they accord with the wishes and convenience of the community." So too is it in parts of Africa; as instance the Koranna Hottentots: "A chief or captain presides over each clan or *kraal,* being usually the person of greatest property; but his authority is extremely limited, and only obeyed so far as it meets the general approbation." And even among the more politically organized Caffres, there is a kindred restraint. The king "makes laws and executes them according to his sole will. Yet there is a power to balance his in the people: he governs only so long as they choose to obey." They leave him if he governs ill.

In its primitive form, then, political power is the feeling of the community, acting through an agency which it has either informally or formally established. Doubtless, from the beginning, the power of the chief is in part personal: his greater strength, courage, or cunning, enables him in some degree to enforce his individual will. But, as the evidence shows, his individual will is but a small factor; and the authority he wields is proportionate to the degree in which he expresses the wills of the rest.

While this public feeling, which first acts by itself and then partly through an agent, is to some extent the feeling spontaneously formed by those concerned, it is to a much larger extent the opinion imposed on them or prescribed for them. In the first place, the emotional nature prompting the general mode of conduct is derived from ancestors, being a product of all past activities; and, in the second place, the special motives which, directly or indirectly, determine the courses pursued, are induced during early life by seniors, and enlisted on behalf of beliefs and usages which the tribe inherits. The governing sentiment is, in short, mainly the accumulated and organized sentiment of the past.

It needs but to remember the mutilation to which, at a prescribed age, each member of a tribe is subject—the knocking out of teeth, the gashing of the flesh, the tattooing, the submission to torture—it needs but to remember that from these imperative customs there is no escape, to see that the directive force which exists before political agency arises, and which afterward makes the political agency its organ, is the gradually formed opinion of countless preceding generations; or rather, not the opinion, which, strictly speaking, is an intellectual product wholly impotent, but the emotion associated with the opinion. This we everywhere find to be at the outset the chief controlling power.

The notion of the Tupis, that, "if they departed from the customs of their forefathers, they should be destroyed," may be named as a definite manifestation of the force with which this transmitted opinion acts. In one of the rudest tribes of the Indian hills, the Juángs, less clothed even than Adam and Eve are said to have been, the women long adhered to their bunches of leaves in the belief that change was wrong. Of the Koranna Hottentots we read that, "when ancient usages are not in the way, every man seems to act as is right in his own eyes," Though the Damara chiefs "have the power of governing arbitrarily, yet they venerate the traditions and customs of their ancestors." Smith says, "Laws the Araucanians can scarcely be said to have, though there are many ancient usages which they hold sacred and strictly observe." According to Brooke, among the Dyaks custom simply seems to have become the law, and breaking of the custom leads to a fine. In the minds of some clans of the Malagasy, "innovation and injury are. . . inseparable, and the idea of improvement altogether inadmissible."

This control by inherited usages is not simply as strong in groups of men who are politically unorganized, or but little organized, as it is in advanced tribes and nations, but it is stronger. As Sir John Lubbock remarks: "No savage is free. All over the world his daily life is regulated by a complicated and apparently most inconvenient set of customs (as forcible as laws), of quaint prohibitions and privileges.\ Though one of these rude societies appears to be structureless, yet its ideas and usages form a kind of invisible framework for it, serving rigorously to restrain certain classes of its actions. And this invisible framework has been slowly and unconsciously shaped, during daily activities impelled by prevailing feelings and guided by prevailing thoughts, through generations stretching back into the far past.

In brief, then, before any definite agency for social control is developed, there exists a control arising partly from the public opinion of the living and more largely from the public opinion of the dead.

But now let us note definitely a truth implied in some of the illustrations above given the truth that, when a political agency has been evolved, its power, largely dependent on present public opinion, is otherwise almost wholly dependent on past public opinion. The ruler, in part the organ of the wills of those around, is in a still greater degree the organ of the wills of those who have passed away; and his own will, much restrained by the first, is still more restrained by the last.

For his function as regulator is mainly that of enforcing the inherited rules of conduct which embody ancestral sentiments and ideas. Everywhere we are shown this. Among the Arafuras, such decisions as are given by their elders are "according to the customs of their forefathers, which are held in the highest regard." So is it with the Kirghiz: "The judgments of the *bais,* or esteemed elders, are based on the known and universally recognized customs." And in Sumatra "they are governed in their various disputes by a set of long-established customs (*adat*), handed down to them from their ancestors. . . . The chiefs, in pronouncing their decisions, are not heard to say, 'So the law directs,' but 'Such is the custom.'"

As fast as orally-preserved custom passes into written law, the political head becomes still more clearly an agent through whom the feelings of the dead control the actions of the living. That the power he exercises is mainly a power which acts through him, we see clearly on noting how little ability he has to resist it if he wishes to do so. His individual will is practically inoperative save where the overt or tacit injunctions of departed generations leave him free. Thus, in Madagascar, "in cases where there is no law, custom, or precedent, the word of the sovereign is sufficient." Among the East Africans, "the only limit to the despot's power is the *ada,* or precedent." Of the Javans, Raffles writes, "The only restraint upon the will of the head of the government is the custom of the country, and the regard which he has for his character among his subjects," In Sumatra the people "do not acknowledge a right in the chiefs to constitute what laws they think proper, or to repeal or alter their ancient usages, of which they are extremely tenacious and jealous," And how imperative is this conformity to the beliefs and sentiments of progenitors is shown by the fatal results apt to occur from disregarding them. "'The King of Ashantee, although represented as a despotic monarch, . . . is not in all respects beyond control.' He is under 'an obligation to observe the national customs, which have been handed down to the people from remote antiquity; and a practical disregard of this obligation, in the attempt to change some of the customs of their forefathers, cost Osai Quamina his throne.'" Which instance reminds us how commonly, as now among the

Hottentots, as in the past among the ancient Mexicans, and as throughout the histories of civilized peoples, rulers have engaged, on succeeding to power, not to change the established order.

Doubtless the proposition that the political head, simple or compound, is in the main but an agency through which works the force of public feeling, present and past, seems at variance with the many facts showing how great may be the power of a ruling man himself. Saying nothing of a tyrant's ability to take lives for nominal reasons or none at all, to make groundless confiscations, to transfer subjects bodily from one place to another, to exact contributions of money and labor without stint, we are apparently shown by his ability to begin and carry on wars which sacrifice his subjects wholesale, that his single will may override the will of the nation. In what way, then, must the original statement be qualified?

While holding that, in unorganized groups of men, the feeling manifested as public opinion controls political conduct, just as it controls the conduct distinguished as ceremonial and religious; and, while holding that governing agencies, during their early stages, are at once the products of aggregate feeling, derive their powers from it, and are restrained by it, we must admit that these primitive relations become complicated when, by war, small groups are compounded and recompounded into great ones. Where the society is largely composed of subjugated people held down by superior force, the normal relation above described no longer exists. We must not expect to find, in a rule coercively established by an invader, the same traits as in a rule that has grown up from within. Societies formed by conquest may be, and frequently are, composed of two societies, which are in large measure, if not entirely, alien; whence it results that there is no longer anything like such united feeling as can embody itself in a political force derived from the whole community. Under such conditions the political head either derives his power exclusively from the feeling of the dominant part of the community, or else, setting the diverse masses of feeling originated in the upper and lower societies one against the other, is enabled so to make his individual will the chief factor.

After making which qualifications, however, it may still be contended that, ordinarily, nearly all the force exercised by the governing agency originates from the feelings, if not of the whole community, yet of the part which is able to manifest its feelings. Though the opinion of the subjugated and unarmed lower society becomes of little account as a political factor, yet the opinion of the dominant and armed part continues to be the main cause of political action. What we are told of the Congo people, that "the king who reigns as a despot over the people is often disturbed in the exercise of his power, by the princes his vassals"—what we are told of the despotically-governed Dahomans, that "the ministers, war-captains, and feticheers may be, and often are, individually punished by the king: collectively they are too strong for him, and without their cordial cooperation he would soon cease to reign"—is what we recognize as having been true, and as being still true, in various better-known societies, where the power of the supreme head is nominally absolute. From the time when the Roman emperors were chosen by the soldiers and slain when they did not please them, to the present time, when, as we are told of Russia, the desire of the army often determines the will of the Czar, there have been many illustrations of the truth that an autocrat is politically strong or weak according as many or few of the influential classes give him their support; and that even the sentiments of those who are politically prostrate greatly affect the political action: instance the influence of Turkish fanaticism over the decisions of the Sultan.

A number of facts must be remembered if we are rightly to estimate the power of the aggregate will in comparison with the power of the autocrat's will. There is the fact that the autocrat is obliged to respect and maintain the great mass of institutions and laws produced by past sentiments and ideas, which have acquired a religious sanction; so that, as in ancient Egypt, dynasties of despots live and die and leave the social order essentially unchanged. There is the fact that a serious change of the social order, at variance with general feeling, is likely afterward to be reversed, as when, in Egypt, Amenhotep IV, spite of a rebellion, succeeded in establishing a new religion, which was abolished in a succeeding reign; and there is the allied fact that laws much at variance with the general will prove abortive, as, for instance, the sumptuary laws made by mediæval kings, which, continually reënacted, continually failed. There is the fact that, supreme as he may be, and divine as the nature ascribed to him, the all-powerful king is yet shackled by usages which often make his daily life a slavery; the opinions of the living oblige him to fulfill the dictates of the dead. There is the fact that if he does not conform, or if he otherwise produces by his acts much adverse feeling, his servants, civil and military, refuse to act, or turn against him; and in extreme cases there comes an example of "despotism tempered by assassination." And there is the further fact that habitually, in societies where an offending autocrat is from time to time removed, another autocrat is set up; the implication being that the average sentiment is of a kind which not only tolerates but desires autocracy. That, which is by some called loyalty and by others servility, both creates the absolute ruler and gives him the power he exercises.

But the cardinal truth, difficult adequately to appreciate, is that, while the forms and laws of each society are the consolidated products of the emotions and ideas of those who have lived throughout the past, they are made operative by the subordination of existing emotions and ideas to them. We are familiar with the thought of "the dead hand" as controlling the doings of the living in the uses made of property; but the effect of "the dead hand," in ordering life at large through the established political system, is immeasurably greater. That which, from hour to hour, in every country, governed despotically or otherwise, produces the obedience making political action possible, is the accumulated and organized sentiment felt toward inherited institutions, made sacred by tradition. Hence it is undeniable that, taken in its widest acceptation, the feeling of the community is the sole source of political power; in those communities, at least, which are not under foreign domination. It was so at the outset of social life, and it still continues substantially so.

It has come to be a maxim of science that in the causes still at work are to be identified the causes which, similarly at work during past times, have produced the state of things now existing. Acceptance of this maxim and pursuit of the inquiries suggested by it lead to verifications of the foregoing conclusions.

For day after day, every public meeting illustrates afresh this same differentiation characterizing the primitive political agency, and illustrates afresh the actions of its respective parts. There is habitually the great body of the less distinguished, forming the audience, whose share in the proceedings consists in expressing approval or disapproval, and saying ay or no to the resolutions proposed. There is the smaller part, occupying the platform—the men whose wealth, position, or capacity gives them influence—the local chiefs by whom the discussions are carried on. And there is the chosen head, commonly the man of greatest mark to be obtained, who exercises a recognized power over speakers and audience—the temporary king. Even an informally summoned assemblage soon resolves itself into these divisions more or less distinctly; and when the assemblage becomes a permanent body, as of the men composing a commercial company, or a philanthropic society, or a club, definiteness is quickly given to the three divisions—president or chairman, board or committee, proprietors or members. To which add that, though at first, like the meeting of the primitive horde or the modern public meeting, one of these permanent associations, voluntarily formed, exhibits a distribution of powers such that the select few and their head are subordinate to the mass; yet, as circumstances determine, the proportions of the respective powers usually change more or less decidedly. Where the members of the mass are not only much interested in the transactions, but are so placed that they can easily cooperate, they hold in check the select few and their head; but, where wide distribution, as of railway shareholders, hinders joint action, the select few become, in large measure, an oligarchy, and out of the oligarchy there not unfrequently grows an autocrat: the constitution becomes a despotism tempered by revolution.

In saying that from hour to hour proofs occur that the force possessed by a political agency is derived from aggregate feeling, partly embodied in the consolidated system which has come down from the past, and partly excited by immediate circumstances, I do not refer only to the proofs that among ourselves governmental actions are habitually thus determined, and that the actions of all minor bodies, temporarily or permanently incorporated, are thus determined. I refer, rather, to the illustrations of the irresistible control exercised by average sentiment and opinion over conduct at large. Such facts as that, while public opinion is in favor of dueling, law fails to prevent it, and that sacred injunctions, backed by threats of damnation, are powerless to check the most iniquitous aggressions when the prevailing interests and passions prompt them, alone suffice to show that legal codes and religious creeds, with the agencies enforcing them, are impotent in face of an adverse sentiment. On remembering the eagerness for public applause and the dread of public disgrace which stimulate and restrain men, we cannot question that the diffused manifestations of feeling habitually dictate their careers when their immediate necessities have been satisfied. It requires only to contemplate the social code which regulates life down even to the color of an evening necktie, and to note how those who dare not break this code have no hesitation in smuggling, to see that an unwritten law enforced by opinion is more peremptory than a written law not so enforced. And still more on observing that men disregard the just claims of creditors, who for goods given cannot get the money, while they are anxious to discharge so-called debts of honor to those who have rendered neither goods nor services, we are shown that the control of prevailing sentiment, unenforced by law and religion, may be more potent than law and religion together when they are backed by sentiment less strongly manifested. Looking at the total activities of men, we are obliged to admit that they are still, as they were at the outset of social life, guided by the aggregate feeling, past and present; and that the political agency, itself a gradually-developed product of such feeling, continues still to be in the main the vehicle for a specialized portion of it, regulating actions of certain kinds.

Partly, of course, I am obliged here to set forth this general truth as an essential element of political theory. My excuse for insisting at some length on what appears to be a trite conclusion must be, that, however far nominally recognized, it is actually recognized to a very small extent. Even in our own country, where non-political agencies spontaneously produced and worked are many and large, and still more in most other countries less characterized by them, there is no due consciousness of the truth that the combined impulses which work through political agencies can, in the absence of such agencies, produce others through which to work. Politicians reason as though state instrumentalities have intrinsic power, which they have not, and as though the feeling which creates them has not intrinsic power, which it has. Evidently their actions must be greatly affected by reversal of these ideas.

VI. Political Heads – Chiefs, Kings, etc…

Of the three components of the triune political structure traceable at the outset, we have now to follow the development of the first. Already in the last two chapters something has been said, and more has been implied, respecting that most important differentiation which results in the establishment of a headship. What was there indicated under its general aspects has here to be elaborated under its special aspects.

"When Rink asked the Nicobarians who among them was the chief, they replied, laughing, how could he believe that *one* could have power against so many?" I quote this as a reminder that there is at first resistance to the assumption of supremacy by one member of a group—a resistance which, though in some types of men small, is in most considerable, and in a few very great. To instances already given of tribes practically chief-less, may be added, from America, the Haidahs, among whom "the people seemed all equal"; the Californian tribes, among whom "each individual does as he likes"; the Navajos, among whom "each is sovereign in his own right as a warrior"; and from Asia the Angamies, who "have no recognized head or chief, although they elect a spokesman, who, to all intents and purposes, is powerless and irresponsible."

Such small subordination as rude groups show occurs only when the need for joint action is imperative, and control is required to make it efficient. Instead of recalling before-named examples of temporary chieftainship, I may here give a few others. Of the Lower Californians we read, "In hunting and war they have one or more chiefs to lead them, who are selected only for the occasion." Of the Flatheads' chiefs it is said that "with the war their power ceases." Among the Sound Indians the chief "has no authority, and only directs the movements of his band in warlike incursions."

As observed under another head, this primitive insubordination has greater or less play according as the environment and the habits of life hinder or favor coercion. The Lower Californians, above instanced as chief-less, Baegert says resemble "herds of wild swine, which run about according to their own liking, being together to-day and scattered to-morrow, till they meet again by accident at some future time." "The chief among the Chipewyans are now totally without power," says Franklin; and these people exist as small migratory bands. Of the Abipones, who are "impatient of agriculture and a fixed home," and "are continually moving from place to place," Dobrizhoffer writes, "they neither revere their cacique as a master, nor pay him tribute or attendance as is usual with other nations." The like holds under like conditions with other races remote in type. Of the Bedouins Burckhardt remarks, "The sheik has no fixed authority"; and, according to another writer, "A chief who has drawn the bond of allegiance too tight is deposed or abandoned, and becomes a mere member of a tribe, or remains without one."

And now, having noted the original absence of political control, the resistance it meets with, and the circumstances which facilitate evasion of it, we may ask, What causes aid its growth? There are several; and chieftainship becomes settled in proportion as they cooperate.

Among the members of the primitive group, slightly unlike in various ways and degrees, there is sure to be someone who has a recognized superiority. This superiority may be of several kinds, which we will briefly glance at.

Though in a sense abnormal, the cases must be noted in which the superiority is that of an alien immigrant. The head-men of the Khonds "are usually descended from some daring adventurer" of Hindoo blood. Forsyth remarks the like of "most of the chiefs" in the highlands of Central Asia. And the traditions of Bochica among the Chibchas, Amalivaca among the Tamanacs, and Quetzalcoatl among the Mexicans, imply kindred origins of chieftainships. Here, however, we are mainly concerned with superiorities arising within the tribe.

101

The first to be named is that which goes with seniority. Though age, when it brings incapacity, is often among rude peoples treated with such disregard that the old are killed or left to die, yet, so long as capacity remains, the greater experience accompanying age generally insures influence. The chief-less Esquimaux show "deference to seniors and strong men." Burchell says that, over the Bushmen, old men seem to exercise the authority of chiefs to some extent; and the like is true with the natives of Australia. By the Fuegians "the word of an old man is accepted as law by the young people." Each party of Rock Veddahs "has a head-man, the most energetic senior of the tribe," who divides the honey, etc. Even with sundry peoples more advanced the like holds. The Dyaks in north Borneo "have no established chiefs, but follow the counsels of the old man to whom they are related"; and Edwards says of the ungoverned Caribs, that "to their old men, indeed, they allowed some kind of authority."

Naturally, in rude societies, the strong hand gives predominance. Apart from the influence of age, "bodily strength alone procures distinction among" the Bushmen. The leaders of the Tasmanians were tall and powerful men: "Instead of an elective or hereditary chieftaincy, the place of command was yielded up to the bully of the tribe." A remark of Sturt's implies a like origin of supremacy among the Australians. Similarly in South America. Of people on the Tapajos, Bates tells us that "the foot-marks of the chief could be distinguished from the rest by their great size and the length of the stride." And in Bedouin tribes "the fiercest, the strongest, and the craftiest obtains complete mastery over his fellows." During higher stages physical vigor long continues to be an all-important qualification; as in Homeric Greece, where even age did not compensate for decline of strength: "an old chief, such as Peleus and Laertes, cannot retain his position." And throughout mediæval Europe maintenance of headship largely depended on bodily prowess.

Mental superiority, alone or joined with other attributes, is a common cause of predominance. With the Snake Indians, the chief is no more than "the most confidential person among the warriors." Schoolcraft says of the chief acknowledged by the Creeks, that "he is eminent with the people only for his superior talents and political abilities"; and that over the Comanches "the position of a chief is not hereditary, but the result of his own superior cunning, knowledge, or success in war." A chief of the Coroados is one "who, by his strength, cunning, and courage, had obtained some command over them." And the Ostiaks "pay respect, in the fullest sense of the word, to their chief, if wise and valiant; but this homage is voluntary, and not a prerogative of his position."

Yet another source of governmental power in primitive tribes is largeness of possessions; wealth being at once an indirect mark of superiority and a direct cause of influence. With the Tacullies "any person may become a *miuty,* or chief, who will occasionally provide a village feast." "Among the Tolewas, in Del Norte County, money makes the chief." And, of the chief-less Navajos we read that "every rich man has many dependents, and these dependents are obedient to his will, in peace and in war."

But, naturally, in societies not yet politically developed, acknowledged superiority is ever liable to be competed with or replaced by superiority arising afresh. "If an Arab, accompanied by his own relations only, has been successful on many predatory excursions against the enemy, he is joined by other friends; and, if his success still continues, he obtains the reputation of being '*lucky*'; and he thus establishes a kind of second, or inferior, in the tribe." So in Sumatra: "A commanding aspect, an insinuating manner, a ready fluency in discourse, and a penetration and sagacity in unraveling the little intricacies of their disputes, are qualities which seldom fail to procure to their possessor respect and influence, sometimes, perhaps, superior to that of an acknowledged chief." And supplantings of kindred kinds occur among the Tongans and the Dyaks.

At the outset, then, what we before distinguished as the principle of efficiency is the sole principle of organization.

Such political headship as exists is acquired by one whose fitness asserts itself in the form of greater age, superior prowess, stronger will, wider knowledge, quicker insight, or larger wealth. But, evidently, supremacy which thus depends exclusively on personal attributes is but transitory. It is ever liable to be superseded by the supremacy of some more able man from time to time arising; and, if not superseded, is inevitably ended by death. We have, then, to inquire how permanent chieftainship becomes established. Before doing this, however, we must consider more fully the two kinds of superiority which especially conduce to chieftainship, and their modes of operation.

As bodily vigor is a cause of predominance within the tribe on occasions daily occurring, still more on occasions of war is it, when joined with courage, a cause of predominance. War, therefore, ever tends to make more pronounced any authority of this kind which is incipient. Whatever reluctance other members of the tribe have to recognize the leadership of any one member is likely to be overridden by their desire for safety when recognition of his leadership furthers that safety.

This rise of the strongest and most courageous warrior to power is at first spontaneous, and afterward by agreement more or less definite; sometimes joined with a process of testing. Where, as in Australia, each "is esteemed by the rest only according to his dexterity in throwing or evading a spear," it is inferable that such superior capacity for war as is displayed generates of itself such temporary chieftainship as exists. Where, as among the Comanches, anyone who distinguishes himself by taking many "horses or scalps may aspire to the honors of chieftaincy, and is gradually inducted by a tacit popular consent," this natural genesis is clearly shown us. Very commonly, however, there is deliberate choice; as by the Flatheads, among whom, "except by the war-chiefs, no real authority is exercised." By some of the Dyaks, both strength and courage are tested. "The ability to climb lap a large pole, well greased, is a necessary qualification of a fighting chief among the Sea Dyaks"; and St. John says that, in some cases, it was a custom, in order to settle who should be chief, for the rivals to go out in search of a head, the first in finding one being victor.

Moreover, the need for an efficient leader tends ever to reëstablish chieftainship where it is only nominal or feeble. Edwards says of the Caribs that, "in war, experience had taught them that subordination was as requisite as courage; they therefore elected their captains in their general assemblies with great solemnity," and "put their pretensions to the proof with circumstances of outrageous barbarity." Similarly, "although the Abipones neither fear their cacique as a judge, nor honor him as a master, yet his fellow-soldiers follow him as a leader and governor of the war, whenever the enemy is to be attacked or repelled."

These and like facts, of which there are abundance, have three kindred implications. One is that continuity of war conduces to permanence of chieftainship. A second is that, with increase of his influence as successful military head, the chief gains influence as political head. A third is that there is thus initiated a union, maintained through subsequent phases of social evolution, between military supremacy and political supremacy. Not only among the uncivilized Hottentots, Malagasy, and others is the chief or king head of the army—not only among such semi-civilized peoples as the ancient Peruvians and Mexicans do we find the monarch one with the commander-in-chief, but the histories of extinct and surviving nations all over the world exemplify the connection. In Egypt, "in the early ages, the offices of king and general were inseparable." Assyrian records represent the political head as also the conquering soldier; as do the records of the Hebrews. Civil and military supremacy were united among the Homeric Greeks; and in primitive Rome "the general was ordinarily the king himself." That throughout European history it has been so, and partially continues so even now in the more militant societies, needs no showing.

How command of a wider kind follows military command we cannot readily see in societies which have no records; we can but infer that, along with increased power of coercion which the successful head warrior gains, naturally goes the exercise of a stronger rule in civil affairs. That this has been so among peoples who have histories there is proof. Of the primitive Germans Sohm remarks that the Roman invasions had one result: "The kingship became united with the leadership (become permanent) of the army, and, as a consequence, raised itself to a *power* [institution] in the state. The military subordination under the king-leader furthered political subordination under the king. . . . Kingship after the invasions is a kingship clothed with supreme rights—a kingship in our sense." In like manner it is observed by Ranke that, during the wars with the English in the fifteenth century, "the French monarchy, while struggling for its very existence, acquired at the same time, and as the result of the struggle, a firmer organization. The expedients adopted to carry on the contest grew, as in other important cases, to national institutions." And modern instances of the relation between successful militancy and the strengthening of political control are furnished by the career of Napoleon and the recent history of the German Empire.

Political headship, then, commonly beginning with the influence gained by the strongest, most courageous, and most astute warrior, becomes established where activity in war gives opportunity for his superiority to show itself and to generate subordination; and thereafter the growth of political power continues primarily related to the exercise of militant functions.

Very erroneous, however, would be the idea formed if no further origin for political headship were named. There is a kind of influence, in some cases operating alone and in other cases cooperating with that above specified, which is all-important. I mean the influence possessed by the medicine-man.

That this arises as early as the other can scarcely be said; since, until the ghost-theory takes shape, there is no origin for it. But, when belief in the spirits of the dead becomes current, the medicine-man, professing ability to control them and inspiring faith in his pretensions, is regarded with a fear which prompts obedience. When we read of the Thlinkeets that "the supreme feat of a conjurer's power is to throw one of his liege spirits into the body of one who refuses to believe in his power, upon which the possessed is taken with swooning and fits," we may imagine the dread he excites and the sway he consequently gains. From some of the lowest races upward we find illustrations. Fitzroy says of the "doctor-wizard among the Fuegians" that he is the most cunning and most deceitful of his tribe, and that he has great influence over his companions. "Though the Tasmanians were free from the despotism of rulers, they were swayed by the counsels, governed by the arts, or terrified by the fears of certain wise men or doctors. These could not only mitigate suffering but inflict it." A chief of the Haidahs "seems to be the principal sorcerer, and indeed to possess little authority save from his connection with the preterhuman powers." The Dakota medicine-men "are the greatest rascals in the tribe, and possess immense influence over the minds of the young, who are brought up in the belief of their supernatural powers. . . . The war-chief who leads the party to war is always one of these medicine-men, and is believed to have the power to guide the party to success, or save it from defeat." Among more advanced peoples in Africa, supposed powers of working supernatural effects similarly give influence, strengthening authority otherwise gained. It is so with the Amazulu: a chief "practices magic on another chief before fighting with him"; and his followers have great confidence in him if he has much repute as a magician. Hence the power possessed by Langalibalele, who, as Bishop Colenso says, "knows well the composition of that *intelezi* [used for controlling the weather]; and he knows well, too, the war-medicine, i. e., its component parts, being himself a doctor." Still better is seen the governmental influence thus acquired in the case of the king of Obbo, who in time of drought calls his subjects together and explains to them "how much he regrets that their conduct has compelled him to afflict them with unfavorable weather, but that it is their own fault. . . . He must have goats and corn. 'No goats, no rain; that's our contract, my friends,' says Katchiba. . . . Should his people complain of too much rain, he threatens to pour storms and lightning upon them for ever, unless they bring him so many hundred baskets of corn, etc. . . . His subjects have the most thorough confidence in his power," And the king is similarly supposed to have power over the weather among the people of Loango.

A like connection is traceable in the records of various extinct peoples in both hemispheres. Of Huitzilopochtli, the founder of the Mexican power, we read that "a great wizard he had been, and a sorcerer"; and every Mexican king on ascending the throne had to swear "to make the sun go his course, to make the clouds pour down rain, to make the rivers run, and all fruits to ripen." Reproaching his subjects for want of obedience, a Chibcha ruler told them they knew that "it was in his power to afflict them with pestilence, smallpox, rheumatism, and fever, and to make to grow as much grass, vegetables, and plants as they wanted." Ancient Egyptian records yield indications of a similar early belief. Thothmes III, after being deified, "was considered as the luck-bringing god of the country, and a preserver against the evil influence of wicked spirits and magicians." And it was thus with the Jews: "Rabbinical writers are never weary of enlarging upon the magical power and knowledge of Solomon. He was represented as not only king of the whole earth, but also as reigning over devils and evil spirits, and having the power of expelling them from the bodies of men and animals, and also of delivering people to them." The traditions of European peoples furnish kindred evidence. As before shown, stories in the "Heims-kringla Saga" imply that the Scandinavian ruler, Odin, was a medicine-man; as were also Niot and Frey, his successors. And after recalling the supernatural weapons and supernatural achievements of early heroic kings, we can scarcely doubt that with them were in some cases associated the supposed magical powers whence have descended the supposed powers of kings to cure diseases by touching or otherwise. We shall the less doubt this on finding that like powers were ascribed to subordinate rulers of early origin. There were certain ancient Breton nobles whose spittle and touch had curative properties.

One important factor, then, in the genesis of political headship, originates with the ghost-theory, and the concomitant rise of a belief that some men, having acquired power over ghosts, can obtain their aid. Generally the chief and the medicine-man are separate persons; and there then exists between them some conflict: they have competing authorities. But, where the ruler unites with his power, naturally gained, this ascribed supernatural power, his authority is necessarily much increased. Recalcitrant members of his tribe, who might dare to resist him if bodily prowess alone could decide the struggle, do not dare to do this if they believe he can send one of his *posse comitatus* of ghosts to torment them. That rulers desire to unite the two characters we have, in one case, distinct proof. Canon Callaway tells us that, among the Amazulu, a chief will endeavor to discover a medicineman's secrets and afterward kill him.

Still there recurs the question. How does permanent political headship arise? Such political headship as results from bodily power, or courage, or sagacity, even when strengthened by supposed supernatural aid, ends with the life of any savage who gains it. The principle of efficiency, physical or mental, while it tends to produce a temporary differentiation into ruler and ruled, does not suffice to produce a permanent differentiation. There has to cooperate another principle, to which we now pass.

Already we have seen that even in the rudest groups age gives some predominance. Among both Fuegians and Australians, not only old men, but old women, exercise authority. And that this respect for age, apart from other distinction, is an important factor in establishing political subordination, is implied by the curious fact that, in sundry advanced societies characterized by extreme governmental coercion, the respect due to age takes precedence of all other respect. Sharpe remarks of ancient Egypt that "here as in Persia and Judea the king's mother often held rank above his wife." In China, notwithstanding the inferior position of women socially and domestically, there exists this supremacy of the female parent, second only to that of the male parent; and the same thing occurs in Japan. As supporting the inference that subjection to parents prepares the way for subjection to rulers, I may add a converse fact. Of the Coroados, whose groups are so incoherent, we read that "the *pajé,* however, has as little influence over the will of the multitude as any other, for they live without any bond of social union, neither under a republican nor a patriarchal form of government. Even family ties are very loose among them. . . there is no regular precedency between the old and the young, for age appears to enjoy no respect among them." And, as reënforcing this converse fact, I may add that, as I have shown elsewhere, the Mantras, the Caribs, the Mapuches, the Brazilian Indians, the Gallinomeros, the Shoshones, the Navajos, the Californians, the Comanches, who submit very little or not at all to chiefly rule, display a filial submission which is mostly small and ceases early.

But now under what circumstances does respect for age take that pronounced form seen in societies distinguished by great political subordination? It was pointed out that when men, passing from the hunting stage into the pastoral stage, began to wander in search of food for their domesticated animals, they fell into conditions favoring the formation of that patriarchal group, at once family and miniature society, constituting the unit of composition of societies which reach the highest stages of evolution. We saw that, in the primitive pastoral horde, the man, dissociated from those earlier tribal influences which interfere with paternal power, and which prevent settled relations of the sexes, was so placed as to acquire headship of a coherent group: the father became, "by right of the strong hand, leader, owner, master, of wife, children, and all he carried with him." There were enumerated the influences which tended to make the eldest male a patriarch; and it was shown that not only the Semites, Aryans, and Turanians have exemplified this relation between pastoral habits and the patriarchal organization, but that it recurs in South African races.

Be the causes what they may, however, we find abundant proof that this family supremacy of the eldest male, common among pastoral peoples and peoples who have passed through the pastoral stage into the agricultural stage, naturally develops into political supremacy. Of the Santals Hunter says: "The village government is purely patriarchal. Each hamlet has an original founder (the manjhi-hanan), who is regarded as the father of the community. He receives divine honors in the sacred grove and transmits his authority to his descendants." Of the compound family among the Khonds we read in Macpherson that "there it [paternal authority] reigns nearly absolute. It is a Khond's maxim that a man's father is his god, disobedience to whom is the greatest crime; and all the members of a family live united in strict subordination to its head until his death." And the growth of groups thus arising, into compound and doubly compound groups, acknowledging the authority of one who unites family headship with political headship, has been made familiar by Sir Henry Maine and others as common to early Greeks, Romans, Teutons, and as still affecting social organization among Hindoos and Slavs.

Here, then, we have making its appearance a factor which conduces to permanence of political headship. As was pointed out in a foregoing chapter, while succession by efficiency gives plasticity to social organization, succession by inheritance gives it stability. No settled arrangement can arise in a primitive community so long as the function of each unit is determined exclusively by his fitness; since, at his death, the arrangement, in so far he was a part of it, must be recommenced. Only when his place is forthwith filled by one- whose claim is admitted, does there begin a differentiation which survives through successive generations. And evidently in the earlier stages of social evolution, while the coherence is small and the want of structure great, it is requisite that the principle of inheritance should, especially in respect of the political headship, predominate over the principle of efficiency. Contemplation of the facts will make this clear.

Two primary forms of hereditary succession have to be considered. The system of kinship through females, common among rude peoples, results in descent of property and power to brothers or to the children of sisters; while the system of kinship through males, general among advanced peoples, results in descent of property and power to sons or daughters. We have first to note that succession through females results in less stable political headships than does succession through males.

From the fact named, when treating of the domestic relations, that the system of kinship through females arises where unions of the sexes are temporary or unsettled, it is to be inferred that this system characterizes societies which are unadvanced in all ways, political included. We saw that irregular connections involve paucity and feebleness of known relationships, and a type of family the successive links of which are not strengthened by so many collateral links. A common consequence is, that along with descent through females there goes either no chieftainship, or chieftainship is established by merit, or, if hereditary it is usually unstable. The Australians and Tasmanians may be named as typical instances. Among the Haidahs and other savage peoples of Columbia "rank is nominally hereditary, for the most part by the female line"; and actual chieftainship "depends to a great extent on wealth and ability in war." Of other North American tribes, the Chippewas, Comanches, and Snakes, show us the system of kinship through females joined with either absence of hereditary chieftainship or very feeble development of it. Passing to South America, the Arawaks and the Waraus may be instanced as having female descent and almost nominal though hereditary chiefs; and much the same may be said of the Caribs.

A group of facts having much significance may now be noted. In many societies where descent of property and rank in

112

the female line is the rule, an exception is made in the case of the political head; and the societies exemplifying this exception are societies in which political headship has become relatively stable. Though in Feejee there is kinship through females, yet, according to Seemann, the ruler, chosen from the members of the royal family, is "generally the son" of the late ruler. In Tahiti, where the two highest ranks follow the primitive system of descent, male succession to rulership is so pronounced that, on the birth of an eldest son, the father becomes simply a regent on his behalf. And among the Malagasy, along with a prevailing kinship through females, the sovereign either nominates his successor, or, failing this, the nobles appoint, and, "unless positive disqualification exists, the eldest son is usually chosen." Africa furnishes evidence of varied kinds. Though the Congo people, the coast negroes, and the inland negroes, have formed societies of some size and complexity, notwithstanding that kinship through females obtains in the succession to the throne, yet we read of the first that allegiance is "vague and uncertain"; of the second, that, save where free in form, the government is "an insecure and short-lived monarchic despotism"; and of the third, that, where the government is not of mixed type, it is "a rigid but insecure despotism." Meanwhile, in the two most advanced and powerful states, stability of political headship goes along with departure, partial or complete, from succession through females. In Ashantee the order of succession is "the brother, the sister's son, the son"; and in Dahomey there is male primogeniture. Further instances of this transition are yielded by extinct American civilizations. Though the Aztec conquerors of Mexico brought with them the system of kinship through females, and consequent law of succession, yet this law of succession was partially, or completely, changed to succession through males. In Tezcuco and Tlacopan (divisions of Mexico) the eldest son inherited the kingship; and in Mexico the choice of a king was limited to the sons and brothers of the preceding king. Then, of ancient Peru, Gomara says, "Nephews inherit, and not sons, except in the case of the

113

Incas": this exception in the case of the Incas having the strange peculiarity that "the first-born of this brother and sister [i. e., the Inca and his principal wife] was the legitimate heir to the kingdom"—an arrangement which made the line of descent unusually narrow and definite. And here we are brought back to Africa by the parallelism between the case of Peru and that of Egypt. "In Egypt it was maternal descent that gave the right to property and to the throne. The same prevailed in Ethiopia. If the monarch married out of the royal family, the children did not enjoy a legitimate right to the crown." When we add the statement that the monarch was "supposed to be descended from the gods, in the male and female line," and when we join with this the further statement that there were royal marriages between brother and sister, we see that like causes worked like effects in Egypt and in Peru. For in Peru the Inca was of supposed divine descent; inherited his divinity on both sides; and married his sister to keep the divine blood unmixed. And in Peru as in Egypt there resulted royal succession in the male line, where, otherwise, succession through females prevailed.

With this process of transition from the one law of descent to the other, implied by these last facts, may be joined some processes which preceding facts imply. In New Caledonia a "chief nominates his successor, if possible, in a son or brother": the one choice implying descent in the male line and the other being consistent with descent in either male or female line. And in Madagascar, where the system of female kinship prevailed, "the sovereign nominated his successor—naturally choosing a son." Further, it is to be noted that, where, as in these cases, when no nomination has been made, the nobles choose among members of the royal family, and are determined in their choice by eligibility, there may be, and naturally is, a departure from descent in the female line; and this once broken through is likely, for several reasons, to be abolished. We are also introduced to another transitional process. For some of these cases are among the many in which succession to rulership is fixed in respect of the family, but not fixed in respect of the member of the family—a stage implying

114

a partial but incomplete stability of the political headship. Several instances occur in Africa. "The crown of Abyssinia is hereditary in one family, but elective in the person," says Bruce. "Among the Timmanees and Bulloms, the crown remains in the same family, but the chief or headmen of the country, upon whom the election of a king depends, are at liberty to nominate a very distant branch of that family." And a Caffre "law requires the successor to the king should be chosen from among some of the youngest princes." In Java and Samoa, too, while succession to rulership is limited to the family, it is but partially settled with respect to the individual.

That stability of political headship is secured by establishment of descent in the male line is, of course, not alleged. The assertion simply is, that succession after this mode conduces better than any other to its stability. Of probable reasons for this, one is that in the patriarchal group, as developed among those pastoral races from which the leading civilized peoples have descended, the sentiment of subordination to the eldest male, fostered by circumstances in the family and in the gens, becomes instrumental to a wider subordination in the larger groups eventually formed. Another probable reason is, that with descent in the male line there is more frequently a union of efficiency with supremacy. The son of a great warrior, or man otherwise capable as a ruler, is more likely to possess kindred traits than is the son of his sister; and, if so, it will happen that in those earliest stages, when personal superiority is requisite as well as legitimacy of claim, succession in the male line will conduce to maintenance of power by making usurpation more difficult.

There is, however, a more potent influence which aids in giving permanence to political headship, and which operates more in conjunction with descent through males than in conjunction with descent through females—an influence probably of greater importance than any other.

When showing how respect for age generates patriarchal authority where descent through males has arisen, I gave cases which incidentally showed a further result; namely, that the dead patriarch, worshiped by his descendants, becomes a family deity. In sundry chapters of Vol. I were set forth at length the proofs, past and present, furnished by many places and peoples, of this genesis of gods from propitiated ghosts. Here there remains to be pointed out the strengthening of political headship inevitably thus effected.

Descent from a ruler who when alive was distinguished by superiority, and whose ghost, specially feared, comes to be propitiated in so unusual a degree as to distinguish it from ancestral ghosts at large, exalts and supports the living ruler in two ways. In the first place, he is assumed to inherit from his great progenitor more or less of the character, apt to be considered supernatural, which gave him his power; and, in the second place, making sacrifices to this great progenitor, he is supposed to maintain such relations with him as insure divine aid. Passages in Canon Callaway's account of the Amazulu show the influence of this belief. It is said, "The itongo [ancestral ghost] dwells with the great man, and speaks with him"; and then it is also said, referring to a medicine-man: "The chiefs of the house of Uzulu used not to allow a mere inferior to be even said to have power over the heaven; for it was said that the heaven belonged only to the chief of that place." These facts yield us a definite interpretation of others, like the following, which show that the authority of the terrestrial ruler is increased by his supposed relation to the celestial ruler; be the celestial the ghost of the remotest known ancestor who founded the society, or of a conquering invader, or of a superior stranger.

Of the chiefs among the Kukis, who are descendants of Hindoo adventurers, we read: "All these rajahs are supposed to have sprung from the same stock, which it is believed originally had connection with the gods themselves; their persons are therefore looked upon with the greatest respect and almost superstitious veneration, and their commands are in every case law." Of the Tahitians Ellis says: "The god and the king were generally supposed to share the authority over the mass of mankind between them. The latter sometimes impersonated the former. . . . The kings, in some of the islands, were supposed to have descended from the gods. Their persons were always sacred." According to Mariner, "*Toritonga* and *Veachi* (hereditary divine chiefs in Tonga) are both acknowledged descendants of chief gods who formerly visited the islands of Tonga." And, in ancient Peru, "the Inca gave them (his vassals) to understand that all he did with regard to them was by an order and revelation of his father, the Sun."

This reenforcement of natural power by supernatural power becomes extreme where the ruler is at once a descendant of the gods and himself a god; a union of attributes which is familiar among peoples who do not distinguish between the divine and the human as we do. It was thus in the case just instanced— that of the Peruvians. It was thus with the ancient Egyptians. The monarch "was the representative of the Divinity on earth, and of the same substance"; and not only did he in many cases become a god after death, but he was worshiped as a god during life; as witness the following prayer to Rameses II:

When they had come before the king. . . they fell down to the ground, and with their hands they prayed to the king. They praised this divine benefactor, . . . speaking thus: "We are come before thee, the lord of heaven, lord of the earth, sun, life of the whole world, lord of time, . . . lord of prosperity, creator of the harvest, fashioner and former of mortals, dispenser of breath to all men; animater of the whole company of the gods, . . . thou former of the great, creator of the small, . . . thou our lord, our sun, by whose words out of his mouth Tum lives, . . . grant us life out of thy hands . . . and breath for our nostrils."

This prayer introduces us to a remarkable parallel. Rameses, whose powers, demonstrated by his conquests, were regarded as so transcendent, is here described as ruling not only the lower world but also the upper world; and a like royal power is alleged in two existing societies where absolutism is similarly unmitigated—China and Japan, As shown when treating of "Ceremonial Institutions," both the Emperor of China and the Japanese Mikado have such supremacy in heaven that they promote its inhabitants from rank to rank at will.

That this strengthening of political headship, if not by ascribed godhood then by ascribed descent from a god (either the apotheosized ancestor of the tribe or one of the elder deities), was exemplified among the early Greeks, needs not be shown. It was exemplified, too, among the Northern Aryans. "According to the old heathen faith, the pedigree of the Saxon, Anglian, Danish, Norwegian, and Swedish kings probably also those of the German and Scandinavian kings generally—was traced to Odin, or to some of his immediate companions or heroic sons."

It is further to be noticed that a god-descended ruler who is also chief priest of the gods (as he habitually is) obtains a more effectual supernatural aid than does the ruler to whom magical powers alone are ascribed. For in the first place the invisible agents invoked by the magician are not conceived to be those of highest rank; whereas the divinely-descended ruler is supposed to get the help of a supreme invisible agent. And, in the second place, the one form of influence over these dreaded superhuman beings tends much less than the other to become a permanent attribute of the ruler. Though among the Chibchas we find a case in which magical power was transferred to a successor—though "the cacique of Sogamoso made known that he [Bochica] had left him heir of all his sanctity, and that he had the same power of making rain when he liked," and giving health or sickness (an assertion believed by the people)—yet this is an exceptional case. Speaking generally, the chief whose relations with the supernatural world are those of a sorcerer does not transmit his relations; and he does not, therefore, establish a supernatural dynasty, as does the chief of divine descent.

And now, having considered the several factors which coöperate to establish political headship, let us consider the process of cooperation through its ascending stages. The truth to be noted is, that the successive phenomena which occur in the simplest groups habitually recur in the same order in compound groups, and again in doubly compound groups.

As, in the simple group, there is at first a state in which there is no headship, so, when simple groups which have political heads possessing slight authorities are associated, there is at first no headship of the cluster. The Chinooks furnish an example. Describing them, Lewis and Clarke say: "As these families gradually expand into bands, or tribes, or nations, the paternal authority is represented by the chief of each association. This chieftain, however, is not hereditary." And then comes the further fact, which here specially concerns us, that "the chiefs of the separate villages are independent of each other": there is no general chieftainship.

As headship in the simple group, at first temporary, ceases when the war which initiates it ends, so, in the cluster of groups which severally have recognized heads, a common headship at first results from a war, and lasts no longer than the war. Falkner says, "In a general war, when many nations enter into an alliance against a common enemy," the Patagonians "chose an *apo,* or commander-in-chief, from among the oldest or most celebrated of the caciques." The Indians of the upper Orinoco live "in hordes of forty or fifty under a family government, and they recognize a common chief only in times of war." So is it in Borneo. "During war the chiefs of the Sarebas Dyaks give an uncertain allegiance to a head chief, or commander-in chief." It has been the same in Europe. Seeley remarks that the Sabines "seem to have had a central government only in war-time." Again: "Germany had anciently as many republics as it had tribes. Except in time of war, there was no chief common to all, or even to any given confederation."

This recalls the fact indicated when treating of political integration, that the cohesion within compound groups is less than that within simple groups, and again that the cohesion within the doubly compound less than that within the compound. What was there said of cohesion may here be said of subordination; for we find that, when by continuous war a permanent headship of a compound group has been generated, it is less stable than the headships of the simple groups. Often it lasts only for the life of the man who achieves it; as among the Karens and the Maganga, and as among the Dyaks, of whom Boyle says: "It is an exceptional case if a Dyak chief is raised to an acknowledged supremacy over the other chiefs. If he is so raised he can lay no claim to his power except that of personal merit and the consent of his former equals; and his death is instantly followed by the disruption of his dominions." Even when there has arisen a headship of the compound group which lasts beyond the life of its founder, it remains for a long time not equal in stability to the headships of the component groups. Pallas, while describing the Mongol and Calmuck chiefs as having unlimited power over their dependents, says that the khan had in general only an uncertain and weak authority over the subordinate chiefs. Of the Caffres we read: "They are all vassals of the king, chiefs, as well as those under them; but the subjects are generally so blindly attached to their chiefs that they will follow them against the king." Europe has furnished kindred examples. Of the. Homeric Greeks Mr. Gladstone writes: "It is probable that the subordination of the sub-chief to his local sovereign was a closer tie than that of the local sovereign to the head of Greece." And, during the early feudal period in Europe, allegiance to the local ruler was stronger than that to the general ruler.

In the compound group, as in the simple group, the progress toward stable headship is furthered by the transition from succession by choice to succession by inheritance. During early stages of the simple tribe, chieftainship, when not acquired by individual superiority tacitly yielded to, is acquired by election. In North America it is so with the Aleuts, the Comanches, and many more; in Polynesia it is so with the Land Dyaks; and, before the Mohammedan conquest, it was so in Java. Among the hill-races of India it is so with the Nagas and others. In some regions the transition to hereditary succession is shown by different tribes of the same race. Of the Karens we read that "in many districts the chieftainship is considered hereditary, but in more it is elective." Some Chinook villages have chiefs who inherit their powers, though mostly they are chosen.

Similarly, the compound group is at first ruled by an elected head. Sundry examples come to us from Africa. Bastian says that "in many parts of the Congo region the king is chosen by the petty princes." The crown of Yariba is not hereditary—"the chiefs invariably electing, from the wisest and most sagacious of their own body." And the King of Ibu, says Allen, seems to be "elected by a council of sixty elders, or chiefs of large villages." In Asia it is thus with the Kukis: "One, among all the rajahs of each class, is chosen to be the Prudham or chief rajah of that clan. The dignity is not hereditary, as is the case with the minor rajahships, but is enjoyed by each rajah of the clan in rotation." So has it been in Europe. Though by the early Greeks hereditary right was in a considerable measure recognized, yet the case of Telemachus implies "that a practice, either approaching to election, or in some way involving a voluntary action on the part of the subjects, or of a portion of them, had to be gone through." The like is true of ancient Rome. That the monarchy was elective "is proved by the existence in later times of an office of *interrex,* which implies that the kingly power did not devolve naturally upon an hereditary successor." Later on it was thus with Western peoples. Up to the beginning of the tenth century "the formality of election subsisted. . . in every European kingdom; and the imperfect right of birth required a ratification by public assent." And it was once thus with ourselves. Among the early English the bretwaldship, or supreme headship over the minor kingdoms, was at first elective; and the form of election continued long traceable in our history.

The stability of the compound headship, made greater by efficient leadership in war and by establishment of hereditary succession, is further increased when there coöperates the additional factor—supernatural origin or supernatural sanction. Everywhere, up from a New Zealand king who is strictly *tapu,* or sacred, we may trace this influence; and occasionally, where divine descent or magical powers are not claimed, there is a claim to origin that is more than human. Asia yields an example in the Fodli dynasty, which reigned a hundred and fifty years in south Arabia—a six-fingered dynasty, regarded with awe by the people because of its continuously-inherited malformation. Europe of the Merovingian period yields an example. In pagan times the king's race had an alleged divine origin; but in Christian times, says Waitz, as they could no longer mount back to the gods, the myth still clung to the supernatural: "A sea-monster ravished the wife of Chlogio as she sat by the seashore, and from this embrace Merovech sprang." Later days show us the gradual acquisition of a sacred or semi-supernatural character where it did not originally exist. Divine assent to their supremacy was alleged by the Carlovingian kings. During the later feudal age, rare exceptions apart, kings "were not far removed from believing themselves near relatives of the masters of heaven. Kings and gods were colleagues." In the seventeenth century this belief was justified by divines. "Kings," says Bossuet, "are gods, and share in a manner the divine independence."

So that the headship of a compound group, first arising temporarily during war, becoming with frequent cooperation of the groups settled for life, by election, passing presently into the hereditary form, and becoming more stable as fast as the law of succession becomes well defined and undisputed, acquires its greatest stability only when the king becomes a deputy-god, or when, if his supposed godlike nature is not, as in primitive societies, derived from alleged divine descent, it is replaced by a divine commission guaranteed by ecclesiastical authority.

Where the political head has acquired this absoluteness which results from supposed divine nature, or divine descent, or divine commission, there is naturally no limit to his sway. In theory, and often to a large extent in practice, he is owner of his subjects and of the territory they occupy.

Where militancy is pronounced and the claims of a conqueror unqualified, it is indeed to a considerable degree thus with those uncivilized peoples who do not ascribe supernatural characters to their rulers. Among the Zooloo Caffres the chief "exercises supreme power over the lives of his people"; "the Bheel chiefs have a power over the lives and property of their own subjects"; and in Feejee the subject is property. But it is still more thus where the ruler is considered more than human. Astley tells us that in Loango the king is "called *samba* and *pongo,* that is, god"; and, according to Proyart, the Loango people "say their lives and goods belong to the king," In Wasoro, East Africa, "the king has unlimited power of life and death. . . in some tribes. . . he is almost worshiped." In Msambara the people say, "We are all slaves of the Zumbe (king), who is our Mulungu" (god). "By the state law of Dahomey, as at Benin, all men are slaves to the king, and most women are his wives"; and in Dahomey the king is called "the spirit." The Malagasy speak of the king as "our god"; and he is lord of the soil, owner of all property, and master of his subjects. Their time and services are at his command." In the Sandwich Islands the king, personating the god, utters oracular responses; and his power "extends over the property, liberty, and lives of his people." Various Asiatic rulers, whose titles ascribe to them divine descent and nature, stand in like relations to their peoples. In Siam "the king is master not only of the persons but really of the property of his subjects; he disposes of their labor and directs their movements at will." Of the Burmese we read, "Their goods likewise, and even their persons, are reputed his [the king's] property, and on this ground it is that he selects for his concubine any female that may chance to please his eye." In China "there is only one who possesses authority—the Emperor. . . . A wang, or king, has no hereditary possessions, and lives upon the salary vouchsafed by the Emperor. . . . He is the only possessor of the landed property."

Of course, where unlimited power is possessed by the political head—where, as victorious invader, his subjects lie at his mercy, or where, as divinely descended, his will may not be questioned without impiety, or where he unites the characters of conqueror and god—he naturally absorbs every kind of authority; he is at once military head, legislative head, judicial head, ecclesiastical head. The fully developed king is the supreme center of every social structure and the director of every social function.

In a small tribe it is practicable for the chief personally to discharge all the duties of his office. Besides leading the other warriors in battle, he has time enough to settle disputes, he can sacrifice to the ancestral ghost, he can keep the village in order, he can inflict punishment, he can regulate trading transactions; for those governed by him are but few, and they lie within a narrow space. When he becomes the head of many united tribes, both the increased amount of business and the wider area covered by his subjects put difficulties in the way of exclusively personal administration. It becomes necessary for him to employ others for the purposes of gaining information, conveying commands, and seeing them executed; and, in course of time, the assistants thus employed become established heads of departments with deputed authorities.

While this development of governmental structures in one way increases the ruler's power, by enabling him to deal with more numerous affairs, it in another way decreases his power, for his actions are more and more modified by the instrumentalities through which they are effected. Those who watch the working of administrations, no matter of what kind, have forced upon them the truth that a head regulative agency is at once helped and hampered by its subordinate agencies. In a philanthropic association, a scientific society, or a club, those who govern find that the organized officialism which they have created often impedes, and not unfrequently defeats, their aims. Still more is it so with the immensely larger administrations of the state. Through deputies the ruler receives his information; by them his orders are' executed; and, as fast as his connection with affairs becomes indirect, his control over affairs diminishes; until, in extreme cases, he either lapses into a puppet in the hands of his chief deputy or has his place usurped by him.

Strange as it seems, the two causes which conspire to give permanence to political headship, also, at a later stage, conspire to reduce the political head to an automaton, executing the wills of the agents he has created. In the first place, hereditary succession, when finally settled in some line of descent rigorously prescribed, involves that the possession of supreme power becomes independent of capacity for exercising it. The heir to a vacant throne may be, and often is, too young for discharging its duties; or he may be, and often is, too feeble in intellect, too deficient in energy, or too much occupied with the pleasures which his position offers in unlimited amounts; with the result that in the one case the regent, and in the other the chief minister, becomes the actual ruler. In the second place, that sacred character which he acquires from supposed divine ancestry makes him inaccessible to the ruled. All intercourse with him must be through the agents with whom he surrounds himself. Hence it becomes difficult or impossible for him to learn more than they choose him to know; and there follows inability to adapt his commands to the requirements, and inability to discover whether his commands have been fulfilled. His authority is consequently used to give effect to the purposes of his agents.

Even in so relatively simple a society as that of Tonga, we find an example. There is an hereditary sacred chief who "was originally the sole chief, possessing temporal as well as spiritual power, and regarded as of divine origin," but who is now politically powerless. Abyssinia shows us something analogous. Holding no direct communication with his subjects, and having a sacredness such that even in council he sits unseen, the monarch is a mere dummy. In Gondar, one of the divisions of Abyssinia, the king must belong to the royal house of Solomon, but any one of the turbulent chiefs who has obtained ascendancy by force of arms becomes a Ras—a prime minister or real monarch; but he requires "a titular emperor to perform the indispensable ceremony of nominating a Ras," since the name, at least, of emperor "is deemed essential to render valid the title of Ras." The case of Thibet may be named as one in which the sacredness of the original political head is dissociated from the claim based on hereditary descent; for the Grand Lama, considered as "God the Father," incarnate afresh in each new occupant of the throne, does not receive his divine nature by natural descent, but, receiving it supernaturally, is discovered among the people at large by certain indications of his godhood; and with his divinity, involving disconnection with temporal matters, there goes absence of political power, A like state of things exists in Bootan. "The Dhurma Raja is looked upon by the Bootanese in the same light as the Grand Lama of Thibet is viewed by his subjects—namely, as a perpetual incarnation of the Deity, or Buddha himself in a corporeal form. During the interval between his death and reappearance, or, more properly speaking, until he has reached an age sufficiently mature to ascend his spiritual throne, the office of Dhurma Raja is filled by proxy from among the priesthood." And then along with this sacred ruler there coexists a secular one. Bootan "has two nominal heads, known to us and to the neighboring hill-tribes under the Hindoostanee names of the Dhurma and the Deb Rajas. . . . The former is the spiritual head, the latter the temporal one." Though in this case it is said that the temporal head has not great influence (probably because the priest-regent, whose celibacy prevents him from founding a line, stands in the way of unchecked assumption of power by the temporal head), still the existence of a temporal head implies a partial lapsing of political functions out of the hands of the original political head. But the most remarkable and at the same time most familiar example is that furnished by Japan. Here the supplanting of inherited authority by deputed authority is exemplified, not in the central government alone, but in the local governments. "Next to the prince and his family came the *karos* or 'elders.' Their office became hereditary, and, like the princes, they in many instances became effete. The business of what we may call the clan would thus fall into the hands of any clever man or set of men of the lower ranks, who, joining ability to daring and unscrupulousness, kept the princes and the *karos* out of sight, but, surrounded with empty dignity and commanding the opinion of the bulk of the *samarai* or military class, wielded the real power themselves. They took care, however, to perform every act in the name of the *fainéants,* their lords, and thus we hear of. . . daimios, just as in the case of the Emperors, accomplishing deeds and carrying out policies of which they were perhaps wholly ignorant." This lapsing of political power into the hands of ministers was, in the case of the central government, doubly illustrated. Successors as they were of a god-descended conqueror whose rule was real, the Japanese Emperors gradually became only nominal rulers; partly because of the sacredness which separated them from the nation, and partly because of the early age at which the law of succession frequently enthroned them. Their deputies consequently gained predominance. The regency in the ninth century "became hereditary in the Fujiwara [sprung from the imperial house], and these regents ultimately became all-powerful. They obtained the privilege of opening all petitions addressed to the sovereign, and of presenting or rejecting them at their pleasure." And then, in course of time, this usurping agency had its own authority usurped in like manner. Again succession by fixed rule was rigorously adhered to; and again seclusion entailed loss of hold on affairs. "High descent was the only qualification for office, and unfitness for functions was not regarded in the choice of officials." Besides the Shôgun's four confidential officers, "no one else could approach him. Whatever might be the crimes committed at Kama Koura, it was impossible, through the intrigues of these favorites, to complain of them to the Shôgun." The result was that "subsequently this family. . . gave way to military commanders, who," however, often became instruments in the hands of other chiefs.

Though less definitely, this process was exemplified during early times in Europe. The Merovingian kings, to whom there clung a tradition of supernatural origin, and whose order of succession was so far settled that minors reigned, fell under the control of those who had become chief ministers. Long before Childeric the Merovingian family had ceased really to govern. "The treasures and the power of the kingdom had passed into the hands of the prefects of the palace, who were called 'mayors of the palace,' and to whom the supreme power really belonged. The prince was obliged to content himself with bearing the name of king, having flowing locks and a long beard, sitting on the chair of state, and representing the image of the monarch."

From the evolution standpoint we are thus enabled to discern the relative beneficence of institutions which, considered absolutely, are not beneficent, and are taught to approve as temporary that which, as permanent, we abhor. The evidence obliges us to admit that subjection to despotic rulers has been largely instrumental in advancing civilization. Induction and deduction alike prove this.

If, on the one hand, we group together those wandering, headless hordes, belonging to different varieties of man, which are found here and there over the earth, they show us that, in the absence of political organization, little progress has taken place; and, if we contemplate those settled simple groups which have but nominal heads, we see that, though there is some development of the industrial arts and some coöperation, the degree of advance is but small. If, on the other hand, we glance at those ancient societies in which considerable heights of civilization were first reached, we see them under autocratic rule. In America purely personal government, restricted only by settled customs, characterized the Mexican, Central American, and Chibcha states; and in Peru the absolutism of the divine king was unqualified. In Africa, ancient Egypt exhibited in the most conspicuous manner this connection between despotic control and social evolution. Throughout the distant past it was repeatedly displayed in Asia, from the Accadian civilization downward, and the still extant civilizations of Siam, Burmah, China, and Japan reillustrate it. Early European societies, too, where not characterized by centralized despotism, were still characterized by diffused patriarchal despotism. Only among modern peoples, whose ancestors passed through the discipline given under this social form, and who have inherited its effects, is there arising an habitual dissociation of civilization from subjection to individual will.

The necessity there has been for absolutism is best seen on observing that, in the struggles for existence among societies, those have conquered which, other things equal, were the more subordinate to their chiefs and kings. And, since in early stages military subordination and social subordination go together, it results that, for a long time, the conquering societies continue to be the despotically governed societies. Such exceptions as histories appear to show us really prove the rule. In the conflict between Persia and Greece, the Greeks, but for a mere accident, would have been ruined by that division of councils which results from absence of subjection to a single head. And the habit of appointing a dictator, when in great danger from enemies, implies that the Romans had discovered that efficiency in war requires absoluteness of control.

So that, leaving open the question whether, in the absence of war, primitive groups could ever have developed into civilized nations, we conclude that, under such conditions as there have been, those struggles for existence, among societies which have gone on consolidating smaller into larger until great nations have been produced, necessitated the development of a social type characterized by personal rule of a stringent kind.

To make clear the genesis of this leading political institution, let us set down in brief the several influences which have conspired to effect it, and the several stages passed through.

In the rudest groups, resistance to the assumption of supremacy by any individual habitually prevents the establishment of settled headship, though some influence is commonly acquired by superiority of strength, or courage, or sagacity, or possessions, or the experience which accompanies age.

In such groups, and in tribes somewhat more advanced, two kinds of superiority conduce more than all others to predominance—that of the warrior and that of the medicine-man. Often separate, but sometimes united in the same person, and then greatly strengthening his hands, both these superiorities, tending to initiate political headship, continue thereafter to be important factors in the development of it.

At first, however, the supremacy acquired by a great natural power, or supposed supernatural power, or both, is transitory—ceases with the life of one who has acquired it. So long as the principle of efficiency alone operates, political headship does not become settled. It becomes settled only when there cooperates the principle of inheritance.

The custom of reckoning descent through females, which characterizes many rude societies and survives in others that have made considerable advances, is less favorable to establishment of permanent political headship than is the custom of reckoning descent through males; and, in sundry semi-civilized societies distinguished by permanent political headships, inheritance through males has been established in the ruling house, while inheritance through females survives in the society at large.

Beyond the fact that reckoning descent through males conduces to a more coherent family, to a greater culture of subordination, and to a more probable union of inherited position with inherited capacity, there is the more important fact that it fosters ancestor-worship and the consequent reënforcing of natural authority by supernatural authority. Development of the ghost-theory, leading as it does to special fear of the ghosts of powerful men, until, where many tribes have been welded together by a conqueror, his ghost acquires in tradition the preeminence of a god, produces two effects. In the first place, his descendant, ruling after him, is supposed to partake of his divine nature; and, in the second place, by

130

propitiatory sacrifices to him, is supposed to obtain his aid. Rebellion hence comes to be regarded as alike wicked and hopeless.

The processes by which political headships are established repeat themselves at successively higher stages. In simple groups chieftainship is at first temporary—ceases with the war which initiated it. When simple groups that have acquired permanent political heads unite for military purposes, the general chieftainship is but temporary. As in simple groups chieftainship is at the outset habitually elective, and becomes hereditary at a later stage, so chieftainship of the compound group is at the outset habitually elective, and only later passes into the hereditary. Similarly in some cases where a doubly compound society is formed. Further, this later-established power of a supreme ruler, at first given by election and presently growing hereditary, is commonly less than that of the local rulers in their own localities; and where it becomes greater it is usually by the help of ascribed divine descent or ascribed divine commission.

Where, in virtue of supposed supernatural origin or authority, the king has become absolute, and, owning both subjects and territory, exercises all powers, he is obliged by the multiplicity of his affairs to depute his powers. There follows a reactive restraint due to the political machinery he creates; and this machinery ever tends to become too strong for him. Especially where rigorous adhesion to the rule of inheritance brings incapables to the throne, or where ascribed divine nature causes inaccessibility save through agents, or where both causes conspire, power passes into the hands of deputies. The legitimate ruler becomes an automaton and his chief agent the real ruler, who, in some cases passing through parallel stages, himself becomes an automaton and his subordinates the rulers.

VII. Compound Political Heads

In the preceding chapter on chiefs and kings, we traced the development of the first element in that triune political structure which everywhere shows itself at the outset. We pass now to the development of the second element—the group of leading men among whom the chief is, at first, merely the most conspicuous. Under what conditions this so evolves as to subordinate the other two, what causes make it narrower, and what causes widen it until it passes into the third, we have here to observe.

If the innate feelings and attitudes of a race have large shares in determining the size and cohesions of the social groups it forms, still more must they have large shares in determining the relations which arise among the members of such groups. While the mode of life followed tends to generate this or that political structure, its effects are always complicated by the effects of inherited character. Whether or not the primitive state, in which governing power is equally distributed among all warriors or all elders, passes into the state in which governing power is monopolized by one, depends, in part, on the life of the group as predatory or peaceful, and in part on the natures of its members as prompting them to oppose dictation more or less doggedly. A few facts will make this clear.

The Arafuras (Papuan-Islanders) who "live in peace and brotherly love," have no other "authority among them than the decisions of their elders." Among the harmless Todas "all disputes and questions of right and wrong are settled either by arbitration or by a Punchayet—i. e., a council of five." Of the Bodo and Dhimáls, described as averse to military service, and "totally free from arrogance, revenge, cruelty, and *fierté*," we read that though each of their small communities has a nominal head who pays the tribute on its behalf, yet he is without power, and "disputes are settled among themselves by juries of elders." In these cases, besides absence of the causes which bring about chiefly supremacy, may be noted the presence of causes which directly hinder it. The Papuans generally, typified by the Arafuras above named, while they are described by Modera, Ross, and Kolff, as "good-natured," "of a mild disposition," kind and peaceful to strangers, are said by Earl to be unfit for military action; "their impatience of control. . . utterly precludes that organization which would enable" the Papuans "to stand their ground against encroachments." The Bodo and Dhimáls while "they are void of all violence toward their own people or toward their neighbors," also "resist injunctions, injudiciously urged, with dogged obstinacy." And of a kindred "very fascinating people," the Lepchas, amiable, peaceful, kind, as travelers unite in describing them, and who will not take service as soldiers, we are told that they will "undergo great privation rather than submit to oppression or injustice."

Where the innate tendency to resist coercion is strong, we find this uncentralized political organization maintained, notwithstanding the warlike activities which tend to initiate settled chieftainship. The Nagas "acknowledge no king among themselves, and deride the idea of such a personage among others"; their "villages are continually at feud"; "every man being his own master, his passions and inclinations are ruled by his share of brute force." And then we further find that "petty disputes and disagreements about property are settled by a council of elders, the litigants voluntarily submitting to their arbitration. But, correctly speaking, there is not the shadow of a constituted authority in the Naga community, and, wonderful as it may seem, this want of government does not lead to any marked degree of anarchy and confusion." Similarly among such peoples, remote in type, as many of the warlike tribes of North America. Speaking of these Indians in general, Schoolcraft says that "they all wish to govern, and not to be governed. Every Indian thinks he has a right to do as he pleases, and that no one is better than himself; and he will fight before he will give up what he thinks right." Of the

Comanches, as an example, he remarks that "the democratic principle is strongly implanted in them"; and that for governmental purposes "public councils are held at regular intervals during the year." Further, we read that in districts of ancient Central America there existed somewhat more advanced societies which, though warlike, were impelled by a kindred jealousy to provide against monopoly of power. The government was by an elective council of old men who appointed a war chief; and this war-chief, "if suspected of plotting against the safety of the commonwealth, or for the purpose of securing supreme power in his own hands, was rigorously put to death by the council."

Though the specialities of character which thus lead certain kinds of men in early stages to originate compound political headships, and to resist, even under the stress of war, the rise of single political headships, are innate, we are not without clews to the circumstances which have made them innate; and, with a view to interpretations presently to be made, it will be useful to glance at these. The Comanches and kindred tribes, roaming about in small bands, active and skillful horsemen, have, through long-past periods, been so conditioned as to make coercion of one man by another difficult. So, too, has it been, though in another way, with the Nagas. "They inhabit a rough and intricate mountain-range"; and their villages are perched "on the crests of ridges." Again, very significant evidence is furnished by an incidental remark of Captain Burton to the effect that in Africa, as in Asia, there are three distinctly marked forms of government—military despotisms, feudal monarchies, and rude republics; the rude republics being those formed by "the Bedouin tribes, the hill people, and the jungle races." Clearly, the names of these last show that they inhabit regions which, hindering by their physical characters a centralized form of government, favor a more diffused form of government, and the less decided political subordination which is its concomitant.

These facts are obviously related to certain other facts with which they must be joined. Already evidence has been given that it is relatively easy to form a large society if the country is one within which all parts are readily accessible, while it has barriers through which exit is difficult; and that, conversely, formation of a large society is prevented, or greatly delayed, by difficulties of communication within the occupied area, and by facilities of escape from it. But, as we now see, not only is political integration under its primary aspect of increasing mass hindered by these last-named physical conditions, but there is hindrance to the development of a more integrated form of government. That which impedes social consolidation also impedes the concentration of political power.

The truth here chiefly concerning us, however, is that the continued presence of the one or the other set of conditions fosters a character to which either the centralized or the diffused kind of political organization is appropriate. Existence, generation after generation, in a region where despotic control has arisen, produces an adapted type of nature; partly by daily habit and partly by survival of those most fit for living under such control. Contrariwise, in a region favoring maintenance of their independence by small groups, there is a strengthening, through successive ages, of sentiments averse to restraint; since not only are these sentiments exercised in all by resisting the efforts from time to time made to subordinate them, but, on the average, those who most pertinaciously resist are those who, remaining unsubdued, and transmitting their characters to posterity, determine the tribal character.

Having thus glanced at the effects of the factors, external and internal, as displayed in simple tribes, we shall understand how they cooperate when, by migration or otherwise, such tribes fall into circumstances which favor the growth of large societies.

The case of an uncivilized people of the nature described, who have in recent times shown what occurs when union of small groups into great ones is prompted, will best initiate the interpretation.

The Iroquois nations, each made up of many tribes previously hostile, had to defend themselves against European invaders. Combination for this purpose among these five (and finally six) nations necessitated a recognition of equality of power among them; since agreement to join would not have been arrived at had it been required that some divisions should be subject to others. The groups had to cooperate on the understanding that their "rights, privileges, and obligations" should be the same. Though the numbers of permanent and hereditary sachems appointed by the respective nations to form the Great Council, differed, yet the voices of the several nations were equal. Omitting details of the organization, we have to note first, that for many generations, notwithstanding the wars which this league carried on, its constitution remained stable—no supreme individual arose; and, second, that this equality of power among the groups coexisted with inequality within each group: the people had no share in its government.

A clew is thus furnished to the genesis of those compound headships with which ancient history familiarizes us. We are enabled to see how there came to coexist, in the same societies, some institutions of a despotic kind, with other institutions of a kind appearing to be based on the principle of equality, and often confounded with free institutions. Let us recall the antecedents of those early European peoples who developed governments of this form.

During the wandering pastoral life, subordination to a single head, growing naturally out of fatherhood, was fostered. A recalcitrant member of any group had either to submit to the authority under which he had grown up, or, throwing off its yoke, had to leave the group and face those risks which unprotected life in the desert threatened. The establishment of this subordination was furthered by the more frequent survival of groups in which it was greatest; since, in the conflicts between groups, those of which the members were insubordinate, ordinarily being both smaller and less able to coöperate effectually, were the more likely to disappear. But now, to the fact that in such families and clans circumstances fostered obedience to the father and to the patriarch, has to be added the fact above emphasized, that circumstances also fostered the sentiment of liberty in the relations between clans. The exercise of power by one of them over another was made difficult by wide scattering and by great mobility; and with successful opposition to external coercion, or evasion of it, carried on through numberless generations, the tendency to resent and resist all strange authority was likely to become strong.

Whether, when groups thus disciplined aggregate, they assume this or that form of political organization, depends partly, as already implied, on the conditions into which they fall. Even could we omit those differences between Mongols, Semites, and Aryans, established in prehistoric times by causes unknown to us—even had complete likeness of nature been produced in them by long continuance of pastoral life—yet large societies, formed by combinations of these small ones, could be similar in type only under similar circumstances. Hence, probably, the reason why Mongols and Semites, where they have settled and multiplied, have failed to maintain the autonomies of their hordes after combination of them, and to evolve the resulting institutions. Even the Aryans, among whom chiefly the less concentrated forms of political rule have arisen, yield an illustration. Originally inheriting in common the mental traits generated during their life in the Hindoo-Koosh and its neighborhood, the different divisions of the race have developed different institutions and accompanying characters. Those of them who spread into the plains of India, where great fertility made possible a large population, to the control of which there were small physical impediments, lost their independence of nature, and did not evolve political systems like those which grew up among their Western kindred, under conditions favorable for maintaining the original character.

The implication is, then, that where groups of the patriarchal type fall into regions permitting considerable growth of population, but having physical structures which impede the centralization of power, compound political headships will arise, and for a time sustain themselves, through coöperation of the two factors—independence of local groups and need for union in war. Let us consider some examples.

The island of Crete has numerous high mountain-valleys containing good pasturage, and provides many seats for strongholds—seats which ruins prove that the ancient inhabitants utilized. Similarly with the mainland of Greece. A complicated mountain system cuts off its parts from one another and renders each difficult of access. Especially is this so in the Peloponnesus; and, above all, in the part occupied by the Spartans. It has been remarked that the state which possesses both sides of Taygetus has it in its power to be master of the peninsula: "It is the Acropolis of the Peloponnese, as that country is of the rest of Greece."

When, over the earlier inhabitants, there came the successive waves of Hellenic conquerors, these brought with them the type of nature and organization common to the Aryans, displaying the united traits above described. Such a people, taking possession of such a land, inevitably fell in course of time "into as many independent clans as the country itself was divided by its mountain-chains into valleys and districts." From separation there resulted alienation; so that those remote from one another, becoming strangers, became enemies. In early Greek times the clans, occupying mountain villages, were so liable to incursions from one another that the planting of fruit-trees was a waste of labor. There existed a state like that seen at present among such Indian hill tribes as the Nagas.

Though preserving the tradition of a common descent, and owning allegiance to the oldest male representative of the patriarch, a people spreading over a region which thus cut off from one another even adjacent small groups, and still more those remoter clusters of groups arising in course of generations, would inevitably become disunited in government: subjection to a general head would be more and more difficult to maintain, and subjection to local heads would

138

alone continue practicable. Moreover, there must arise, under such conditions, increasing causes of insubordination, as well as great difficulties in maintaining subordination. When the various branches of a common family spread into localities so shut off from one another as to prevent intercourse, their respective histories, and the lines of descent of their respective heads, must become unknown, or but partially known, to one another; and claims to supremacy made now by this local head and now by that are certain to be disputed. When we remember how, even in settled societies having records, there have been perpetual conflicts about rights of succession, and how, down to our own day, there are frequent lawsuits to decide on heirships to titles and properties, we can not but infer that, in a state like that of the early Greeks, the difficulty of establishing the legitimacy of general headships, conspiring with the desire to assert independence and the ability to maintain it, inevitably entailed lapse into numerous local headships. Of course, under conditions varying in each locality, splittings-up of wider governments into narrower went to different extents; and, naturally, too, reëstablishments of wider governments or extensions of narrower ones in some cases took place. But, generally, the tendency under such conditions must have been to form small independent groups, severally having the patriarchal type of organization. Hence, then, the decay of such kingships as are implied in the "Iliad." As Grote writes, "When we approach historical Greece, we find that (with the exception of Sparta) the primitive, hereditary, unresponsible monarch, uniting in himself all the functions of government, has ceased to reign."

But now what will happen when a cluster of clans of common descent, which have become independent and hostile, are simultaneously endangrered by enemies to whom they are not at all akin, or but remotely akin? Habitually, they will sink their differences and cooperate for defense. But on what terms will they cooperate? Even among friendly groups joint action would be hindered if some claimed supremacy; and, among groups having outstanding feuds, there could be no joint action save on a footing of equality. The common defense would, therefore, be directed by a body formed of the heads of the cooperating small societies; and, if the cooperation for defense were prolonged, or became changed by success into cooperation for offense, this temporary controlling body would tend to become a permanent one holding the small societies together. The special characters of this compound head would, of course, vary with the circumstances. Where the traditions of the united clans agreed in identifying someone chief as the lineal representative of the original patriarch or hero, from whom all descended, precedence and some extra authority would be permitted to him. Where claims derived from descent were disputed, personal superiority or election would determine which member of the compound head should take the lead. If within each of the component groups the power of its chief was unqualified, there would result from union of such chiefs a close oligarchy; while the closeness of the oligarchy would become less in proportion as recognition of the authority of each chief, given by nearness in blood to the divine or semi-divine ancestor, diminished. And in cases where there came to be incorporated numerous aliens, owing allegiance to the heads of none of the component groups, there would come into play influences tending still more to widen the oligarchy.

Such, we may conclude, were the origins of those compound headships of the Greek states which existed at the beginning of the historic period. In Crete, where there survived the tradition of primitive kingship, but where dispersion and subdivision of clans had brought about a condition in which "different towns carried on open feuds," there were "patrician houses, deriving their rights from the early ages of royal government," who continued "to retain possession of the administration." In Corinth, the line of Herakleid kings "subsides gradually, through a series of empty names, into the oligarchy denominated Bacchiadæ. . . . The persons so named were all accounted descendants of Herakles, and formed the governing caste in the city." So was it with Megara. According to tradition, this arose by combination of several villages inhabited by kindred tribes, which, originally in antagonism with Corinth, had probably, in the course of this antagonism, become consolidated into an independent state. And at the opening of the historic period the like had happened in Sikyon and other places. Though in Sparta kingship had survived under an anomalous form, yet the joint representatives of the primitive king, still reverenced because the tradition of their divine descent was preserved, had become little more than members of the governing oligarchy, retaining certain prerogatives. And, though it is true that in its earliest historically-known stage, the Spartan oligarchy did not present the form which would spontaneously arise from the union of the heads of clans for coöperation in war—though it had become elective within a limited class of persons—yet the fact that an age of not less than sixty was a qualification, harmonizes with the belief that it at first consisted of the heads of the respective groups, who were always the eldest sons of the eldest; and that these groups with their heads, described as having been in in pre-Lykurgean times "the most lawless of all the Greeks," became united by that continuous militant life which distinguished them.

The Romans exemplify the rise of a compound headship under conditions which, though partially different from those the Greeks were subject to, were allied fundamentally. In its earliest-known state, Latium was occupied by village-communities, which were united into cantons; while these cantons formed a league headed by Alba—a canton regarded as the oldest and most eminent. This combination was for joint defense; as is shown by the fact that each group of clan-villages composing a canton had an elevated stronghold in common, and also by the fact that the league of cantons had for its center and place of refuge Alba, the most strongly placed as well as the oldest. The component cantons of the league were so far independent that there were wars between them; whence we may infer that when they cooperated for joint defense it was on substantially equal terms. Thus, before Rome existed, the people who formed it had been habituated to a kind of life such that, with great subordination in each family and clan, and partial subordination within each canton (which was governed by a prince, council of elders, and assembly of warriors), there went a union of heads of cantons, who were in no degree subordinate one to another. When the inhabitants of three of these cantons, the Ramnians, Tities, and Luceres, began to occupy the tract on which Rome stands, they brought with them their political organization. The oldest Roman patricians bore the names of rural clans belonging to these cantons. Whether, when seating themselves on the Palatine Hills and on the Quirinal, they preserved their cantonal divisions, is not clear, though it seems probable *a priori*. But, however this may be, there is proof that they fortified themselves against one another, as

well as against outer enemies. The "mount-men" of the Palatine and the "hill-men" of the Quirinal were habitually at feud; and, even among the minor divisions of those who occupied the Palatine, there were dissensions. As Mommsen says, primitive Rome was "rather an aggregate of urban settlements than a single city." And that the clans who formed these settlements brought with them their enmities is to be inferred from the fact that not only did they fortify the hills on which they fixed themselves, but even '* the houses of the old and powerful families were constructed somewhat after the manner of fortresses."

So that again, in the case of Rome, we a see a cluster of small independent communities allied in blood but partially antagonistic, which had to cooperate against enemies on such terms as all would agree to. In early Greece the means of defense were, as Grote remarks, greater than the means of attack; and it was the same in early Rome. Hence, while coercive rule within each family and small group was easy, there was difficulty in extending coercion over many groups— fortified as they were against one another. Moreover, the stringency of government within each settlement constituting the primitive city was diminished by facility of escape from one and admission into another. As we have seen among simple tribes, desertions take place when the rule is unduly harsh; and we may infer that, within each of these clustered settlements, there was a check on exercise of force by the heads of the more powerful families over those of the less powerful, caused by the fear that migration might weaken the settlement and strengthen an adjacent one. Thus the circumstances were such that when, for defense of the primitive city, cooperation became needful, the heads of the clans included in the several settlements came to have substantially equal powers. The original senate was the collective body of clan-elders; and "this assembly of elders was the ultimate holder of the ruling power": it was "an assembly of kings." At the same time, the heads of families in each clan, forming the body of burgesses, stood, for like reasons, on equal footing. Primarily for command in war, there was an elected head, who was also chief magistrate. Though not having the authority given by alleged divine descent, he had the authority given by supposed divine approval; and, himself bearing the insignia of a god, he retained till death the absoluteness appropriate to one. But, besides the fact that the choice, originally made by the senate, had to be again practically made by it in case of sudden vacancy, and besides the fact that each king, nominated by his predecessor, had to be approved by the assembled burgesses, there is the fact that his power was exclusively executive. The assembly of burgesses "was in law superior to, rather than coordinate with, the king." Further, in the last resort was exercised the still superior power of the senate, which was the guardian of the law, and could veto the joint decision of king and burgesses. Thus the constitution was in essence an oligarchy of heads of clans, included in an oligarchy of heads of houses—a compound oligarchy which became unqualified when kingship was suppressed. And here should be emphasized the truth, sufficiently obvious and yet continually ignored, that the Roman Republic, which remained when the regal power ended, was quite alien in nature to those popular governments with which it has been commonly classed. The heads of clans, of which the narrower governing body was formed, as well as the heads of families which formed the wider governing body, were, indeed, jealous of one another's powers; and in so far simulated the citizens of a free state who individually maintain their equal rights. But these heads severally exercised unlimited powers over the members of their households and over their clusters of dependents. A community of which the component groups severally retained their internal autonomies, with the result that the rule within each remained absolute, was nothing but an aggregate of small despotisms. Institutions under which the head of each group, besides owning slaves, had such supremacy that his wife and children, including even married sons, had no more legal rights than cattle, and were at his mercy in life and limb, or could be sold into slavery, can be called free institutions only by those who confound similarity of external outline with similarity of internal structure.

The formation of compound political heads in later times repeats this process in essentials, if not in details. In one way or other the result arises when a common need for defense compels cooperation, while there exists no means of securing cooperation save voluntary agreement.

Beginning with the example of Venice, we notice first that the region occupied by the ancient Veneti included the extensive marshy tract formed of the deposits brought down by several rivers to the Adriatic—a tract which, in Strabo's day, was "intersected in every quarter by rivers, streams, and morasses"; so that "Aquileia and Ravenna were then cities in the marshes." Having for their stronghold this region full of spots accessible only to inhabitants who knew the intricate ways to them, the Veneti maintained their independence, spite of the efforts of the Romans to subdue them, until the days of Cæsar. In later days kindred results were more markedly displayed in that part of this region specially characterized by inaccessibility. From the earliest times the islets, or rather mud-banks, on which Venice stands, were inhabited by a maritime people. Each islet, secure in the midst of its tortuous lagunes, had a popular government of annually elected tribunes. And these original governments, existing at the time when there came several thousands of fugitives, driven from the mainland by the invading Huns, survived under the form of a rude confederation. As we have seen happen in other cases, the union into which these independent little communities were forced for purposes of joint defense was disturbed by feuds; and it was only under the stress of opposition to aggressing Lombards on the one side and Slavonic pirates on the other that a general assembly of nobles, clergy, and citizens appointed a duke or doge to direct the combined forces, and to restrain internal factions; being superior to the tribunes of the united islets and subject only to this body which appointed him. What changes subsequently took place—how, beyond the restraints imposed by the general assembly, the doge was presently put under the check of two elected councilors, and on important occasions had to summon the principal citizens; how there came afterward a representative council, which underwent from time to time changes—does not now concern us. Here we have simply to note that, as in preceding cases, the component groups being favorably circumstanced for severally maintaining their independence of one another, the imperative need for union against enemies initiated a rude compound headship, which, notwithstanding the centralizing effects of war, tended to maintain itself in one or other form.

On finding allied results among men of a different race but occupying a similar region, doubts respecting the process of causation must be dissipated. On the area—half land, half sea—formed of the sediment brought down by the Rhine and adjacent rivers, there early existed scattered families. Living on isolated sand-hills, or in huts raised on piles, they were so secure amid their creeks and mud-banks and marshes, that they remained unsubdued by the Romans. Subsisting at first by fishing, with here and there such small agriculture as was possible, and eventually becoming maritime and commercial, these people, in course of time, rendered their land more habitable by damming out the sea; and they long enjoyed a

145

partial if not complete independence. In the third century "the Low Countries contained the only free people of the German race." Especially the Frisians, more remote than the rest from invaders, "associated themselves with the tribes settled on the limits of the German Ocean, and formed with them a connection celebrated under the title of the "Saxon League."' Though, at a later time, the inhabitants of the Low Countries fell under power of France, yet the nature of their habitat continued to give them such advantages in resisting foreign control that they organized themselves after their own fashion, notwithstanding interdicts. "From the time of Charlemagne the people of the ancient Menapia, now become a prosperous commonwealth, formed political associations to raise a barrier against the despotic violence of the Franks." Meanwhile the Frisians, who, after centuries of resistance to the Franks, were obliged to yield and render small tributary services, retained their internal autonomy. They formed "a confederation of rude but self-governed maritime provinces," each of these seven provinces being divided into districts severally governed by elective heads with their councils, and the whole being under a general elective head and a general council.

Of illustrations which modern times have furnished, must be named those which again show us the effects of a mountainous region. The most notable is, of course, that of Switzerland. Surrounded by forests, "among marshes and rocks and glaciers, tribes of scattered shepherds had, from the early times of, the Roman conquest, found a land of refuge from the successive invaders of the rest of Helvetia." In the labyrinths of the Alps, accessible to those only who knew the ways to them, their cattle fed unseen; and against straggling bands of marauders who might discover their retreats they had great facilities for defense. These districts—which eventually became the cantons of Schwytz, Uri, and Unterwalden, originally having but one common center of meeting, but eventually, as population increased, getting three, and forming separate political organizations—long preserved complete independence. With the spread of feudal subordination throughout Europe, they became nominally subject to the Emperor; but, refusing obedience to the superiors set over them, they entered into a solemn alliance, renewed from time to time, to resist outer enemies. Details of their history need not detain us. The fact of moment is, that in these three cantons, which physically favored in so great a degree the maintenance of independence by individuals and by groups, the people, while framing for themselves free governments, united on equal terms for joint defense. And it was these typical "Swiss," as they were the first to be called, whose union formed the nucleus of the larger unions which, through varied fortunes, eventually grew up. Severally independent as were the cantons composing these larger unions, there at first existed feuds among them, which were suspended during the needs for joint defense. Only gradually did the leagues pass from temporary and unsettled forms to a permanent and settled form. Two facts of significance should be added. One is that, at a later date, a like process of resistance, federation, and emancipation from feudal tyranny, among separate communities occupying small mountain-valleys, took place in the Orisons and in the Valais—regions which, though mountainous, were more accessible than those of the Oberland and its vicinity. The other is that the more level cantons neither so early nor so completely gained their independence; and, further, that their internal constitutions were less free in form. A marked contrast existed between the aristocratic republics of Berne, Lucerne, Fribourg, and Soleure and the pure democracies of the forest cantons and the Orisons; in the last of which a every little hamlet resting in an Alpine valley, or perched on mountain-crag, was an independent community, of which all the members were absolutely equal—entitled to vote in every assembly, and qualified for every public function. . . . Each hamlet had its own laws, jurisdiction, and privileges," the hamlets being federated into communes, the communes into districts, and the districts into a league.

Lastly, with the case of Switzerland may be associated that of San Marino—a little republic which, seated in the

Apennines, and having its center on a cliff a thousand feet high, has retained its independence for fifteen centuries. Here eight thousand people are governed by a senate of sixty, and by captains elected every half year, assemblies of the whole people being called on important occasions. There is a standing army of eighteen, "taxation is reduced to a mere nothing," and officials are paid by the honor of serving.

One noteworthy difference between the compound heads arising under physical conditions of the kinds exemplified, must not be overlooked—the difference between the oligarchic form and the more or less popular form. As shown at the outset of this section, if each of the groups united by militant cooperation is despotically ruled—if the groups are severally framed on the patriarchal type, or are severally governed by men of supposed divine descent—then the compound head becomes one in which the people at large have no share. But if, as in these modern cases, patriarchal authority has decayed; or if belief in divine descent has been undermined by a creed at variance with it; or if peaceful habits have weakened that coercive authority which war ever strengthens—then the compound head is no longer an assembly of petty despots. With the progress of these changes it becomes more and more a head formed of those who exercise power not by right of position but by right of appointment.

There are other conditions which favor the rise of compound heads, temporary if not permanent: those, namely, which occur at the dissolutions of preceding organizations. Among people habituated through countless generations to personal rule, having sentiments appropriate to it, and no conception of anything else, the fall of one despot is at once followed by the rise of another; or, if a large personally-governed empire collapses, its parts severally generate governments for themselves of like kind. But, among less servile peoples, the breaking up of political systems having single heads is apt to be followed by the establishment of others having compound heads; especially where there is a simultaneous separation into parts which have not local governments of stable kinds. Under such circumstances there is a return to the primitive state. The preexisting regulative system having fallen, the members of the community are left without any controlling power save the aggregate will; and, political organization having to commence afresh, the form first assumed is akin to that which we see in the assembly of the savage horde, or in the modern public meeting. Whence there presently results the rule of a select few subject to the approval of the many.

In illustration may first be taken the rise of the Italian republics. When, during the ninth and tenth centuries, the German emperors, who had long been losing their power to restrain local antagonisms in Italy and the outrages of wandering robber bands, failed more than ever to protect their subject communities, and, as a simultaneous result, exercised diminished control over them, it became at once necessary and practicable for the Italian towns to develop political organizations of their own. Though in these towns there were remnants of the old Roman organization, this had obviously become effete; for, in time of danger, there was an assembling of "citizens at the sound of a great bell, to concert together the means for their common defense." Doubtless on such occasions were marked out the rudiments of those republican constitutions which afterward arose. Though it is alleged that the German emperors allowed the towns to form these constitutions, yet we may reasonably conclude, rather, that, having no care further than to get their tribute, they made no efforts to prevent the towns from forming them. And though Sismondi says of the townspeople, "ils cherchèrent à se constituer sur le modèle de la république romaine," yet we may question whether, in those dark days, the people knew enough of Roman institutions to be influenced by their knowledge. With more probability may we infer that "this meeting of all the men of the state capable of bearing arms. . . in the great square," originally called to take measures for repelling aggressors—a meeting which must, at the very beginning, have been swayed by a group of dominant citizens, and must have chosen leaders—was itself the republican government in its incipient form. Meetings of this kind, first occurring on occasions of emergency, would gradually come into use for deciding on all important public questions. Repetition would bring greater regularity in the modes of procedure, and greater definiteness in the divisions formed, ending in compound political heads, presided over by elected chiefs. And that this was the case in those early stages of which there remain but vague accounts, is shown by the fact that a similar, though somewhat more definite, process afterward occurred at Florence, when the usurping nobles were overthrown. Definite records tell us that in 1250 "the citizens assembled at the same moment in the square of Santa Croce; they divided themselves into fifty groups, of which each group chose a captain, and thus formed companies of militia; a council of these officers was the first-born authority of this newly revived republic." Clearly that sovereignty of the people which, for a time, characterized these small governments, would inevitably arise if the political form grew out of the original public meeting; while it would be unlikely to have arisen had the political form been artificially devised by a limited class.

That this interpretation harmonizes with the facts which modern times have furnished, scarcely needs pointing out. On an immensely larger scale and in ways variously modified, here by the slow collapse of an old *régime* and there by combination for war, the rise of the first French Republic and that of the American Republic have similarly shown us this tendency toward resumption of the primitive form of political organization, when a decayed or otherwise incapable government is broken up. Greatly obscured by complicating circumstances and special incidents as these transformations were, we may recognize in them the play of the same general causes.

In the last chapter we saw that, as conditions determine, the first element of the triune political structure may be differentiated from the second in various degrees—beginning with the warrior chief slightly predominant over other warriors, and ending with the divine and absolute king, widely distinguished from the select few next to him. By the foregoing examples we are shown that the second element is, as conditions determine, variously differentiated from the third: being at the one extreme qualitatively distinguished in a high degree and divided from it by an impassable barrier, and at the other extreme almost merged into it.

Here we are introduced to the truth next to be dealt with: that not only do conditions determine the various forms which compound heads assume, but that conditions determine the various changes—they undergo. There are two leading kinds of such changes those through which the compound head passes toward a less popular form, and those through which it passes toward a more popular form. We will glance at them in this order.

Progressive narrowing of the compound head is one of the concomitants of continued military activity. Beginning with the case of Sparta, the constitution of which in its early form differed but little from that which the "Iliad" shows us existed among the Homeric Greeks, we see, in the first place, the tendency toward concentration of power in the regulation, made a century after Lykurgus, that, "in case the people decided crookedly, the senate with the kings should reverse their decisions"; and then we see that later, in consequence of the gravitation of property into fewer hands, "the number of qualified citizens went on continually diminishing": the implication being not only a relatively-increased power of the oligarchy, but, probably, a growing supremacy of the wealthier members within the oligarchy itself. Turning to the case of Rome, ever militant, we find that in course of time inequalities increased to the extent that the senate became "an order of lords, filling up its ranks by hereditary succession, and exercising collegiate misrule"; and then "out of the evil of oligarchy there emerged the still worse evil of usurpation of power by particular families." In the Italian republics, again, perpetually at war one with another, there resulted a kindred narrowing of the governing body. The nobility, deserting their castles, began to direct "the municipal government of the cities, which consequently, during this period of the republics, fell chiefly into the hands of the superior families." Then at a later stage, when industrial progress had generated wealthy commercial classes, these, competing with the nobles for power, and finally displacing them, repeated within their respective bodies this same process. The richer guilds deprived the poorer of their shares in the choice of the ruling agencies; the privileged class was continually narrowed by disqualifying regulations; and newly risen families were excluded by those of long standing. So that, as Sismondi points out, such of the numerous Italian republics as remained nominally such at the close of the fifteenth century were, like "Sienna and Lucca, each governed by a single caste of citizens: . . . had no longer popular governments." A kindred result occurred among the Dutch. During the wars of the Flemish cities with the nobles and with one another, the relatively popular governments of the towns became narrowed. The greater guilds excluded the lesser from the ruling body, and their members "clothed in the municipal purple. . . ruled with the power of an aristocracy; . . . the local government was often an oligarchy, while the spirit of the burghers was peculiarly democratic." And with these illustrations may be joined that furnished by those Swiss cantons which, physically characterized in ways less favorable to individual independence, were at the same time given to wars, offensive as well as defensive. Berne, Lucerne, Fribourg, Soleure, acquired political constitutions in large measure oligarchic; and in "Berne, where the nobles had always been in the ascendant, the entire administration had fallen into the hands of a few families, with whom it had become hereditary."

We have next to note as a cause of progressive modification in compound heads, that, like simple heads, they are apt to be subordinated by their administrative agents. The first case to be named is one in which this effect is exemplified along with the last—the case of Sparta. Originally appointed by the kings to perform prescribed duties, the ephors first made the kings subordinate, and eventually subordinated the senate; so that they became substantially the rulers. From this we may pass to the instance supplied by Venice, where power, once exercised by the people, gradually lapsed into the hands of an executive body, the members of which, habitually reelected, and at death replaced by their children, became an aristocracy, whence there eventually grew the Council of Ten, who were, like the Spartan ephors, "charged to guard the security of the state with a power higher than the law"; and who thus, "restrained by no rule," constituted the actual government. Through its many revolutions and changes of constitution, Florence exhibited like tendencies. The appointed administrators, now signoria, now priors, became able, during their terms of office, to carry out their ends even to the extent of suspending the constitution—getting the forced assent of the assembled people, who were surrounded by armed men. And then, eventually, the head executive agent, nominally reelected from time to time but practically permanent, became, in the person of Cosmo de' Medici, the founder of an inherited headship.

But the liability of the compound political head to become subject to its civil agents, is far less than its liability to become subject to its military agents. From the earliest times this liability has been exemplified and commented upon; and, familiar as it is, I must here illustrate and emphasize it, because it directly bears on one of the cardinal truths of political theory. Setting out with the Greeks we observe, in the first place, that the tyrants, by whom oligarchies were so often overthrown, had armed forces at their disposal. Either the tyrant was "the executive magistrate, upon whom the oligarchy themselves had devolved important administrative powers," or he was a demagogue, who pleaded the alleged interests of the community, "in order to surround" himself "with armed defenders"—soldiers being in either case the agents of his usurpation. And then, in the second place, we see the like done by the successful general. As Macchiavelli remarks of the Romans: "For the further abroad they [the generals] carried their arms, the more necessary such prolongations [of their commissions] appeared, and the more common they became;

hence it arose, in the first place, that but a few of their citizens could be employed in the command of armies, and consequently few were capable of acquiring any considerable degree of experience or reputation; and in the next, that when a commander in chief was continued for a long time in that post, he had an opportunity of corrupting his army to such a degree that the soldiers entirely threw off their obedience to the senate, and acknowledged no authority but his. To this it was owing that Sylla and Marius found means to debauch their armies and make them fight against their country; and that Julius Cæsar was enabled to make himself absolute in Rome."

The Italian republics, again, furnish many illustrations. By the beginning of the fourteenth century, those of Lombardy "all submitted themselves to the military power of some nobles to whom they had intrusted the command of their militias, and thus all lost their liberty." Later times and nearer regions yield instances. At home Cromwell showed how the successful general tends to become autocrat. In the Netherlands the same thing was exemplified by the Van Arteveldes, father and son, and again by Maurice of Nassau; and, but for form's sake, it would be needless to name the case of Napoleon. It should be added that not only by command of armed forces is the military chief enabled to seize on supreme power, but acquired popularity, especially in a militant nation, places him in a position which makes it relatively easy to do this. Neither their own experience, nor the experiences of other nations throughout the past, prevented the French from lately making Marshal MacMahon executive head; and even the Americans, in more than once choosing General Grant for President, proved that, predominantly industrial though their society is, militant activity promptly caused an incipient change toward the militant type, of which an essential trait is the union of civil headship with military headship.

From the influences which tend to narrow compound political headships, or change them into single ones, let us pass to the influences which tend to widen them. The case of Athens is, of course, the first to be considered. To understand

154

this we must remember that, up to the time of Solon, democratic government did not exist in Greece. The only known forms were the oligarchic and the despotic; and in those early days, before political speculation began, it is certain that there was not recognized in theory a social form wholly unknown in practice. We have, therefore, to exclude the notion that popular government arose in Athens under the guidance of any preconceived idea. As having the same implication should be added the fact that—Athens being governed by an oligarchy at the time—the Solonian legislation served but to qualify and broaden the oligarchy and remove crying injustices. In seeking the causes which worked through Solon, and also made practicable the reorganization he initiated, we shall find them to lie in the direct and indirect influences of trade. Grote comments on "the anxiety, both of Solon and of Drako, to enforce among their fellow-citizens industrious and self-maintaining habits"—a proof that, even before Solon's time, there was in Attica little or no reprobation of "sedentary industry, which in most other parts of Greece was regarded as comparatively dishonorable." Moreover, Solon was himself in early life a trader; and his legislation "provided for traders and artisans a new home at Athens, giving the first encouragement to that numerous town-population, both in the city and in the Peiraeus, which we find actually residing there in the succeeding century." The immigrants who flocked into Attica because of its greater security, Solon was anxious to turn rather to manufacturing industry than to cultivation of a soil naturally poor; and one result was "a departure from the primitive temper of Atticism, which tended both to cantonal residence and rural occupation"; while another result was to increase the. number of people who stood outside those gentile and phratric divisions, which were concomitants of the patriarchal type and of personal rule. And then the constitutional changes made by Solon were in leading respects toward industrial organization. The introduction of a property-qualification for classes, instead of a birth-qualification, diminished the rigidity of the political form, since acquirement of wealth by industry, or otherwise,

155

made possible an admission into the oligarchy, or among others of the privileged. By forbidding self-enslavement of the debtor, and by emancipating those who had been self-enslaved, his laws added largely to the enfranchised class as distinguished from the slave-class. In another aspect this change, leaving equitable contracts untouched, prevented those inequitable contracts under which, by a lien on himself, a man gave more than an equivalent for the sum he borrowed. And, with a decreasing number of cases in which there existed the relation of master and slave, went an increasing number of cases in which benefits were exchanged by agreement The odium attaching to that lending at interest which ended in slavery of the debtor having disappeared, legitimate lending became general and unopposed, the rate of interest was free, and accumulated capital was made available. Then, as coöperating cause, and as ever increasing consequence, came the growth of a population favorably circumstanced for acting in concert. Urban people, who, daily in contact, can gather one another's ideas and feelings, and who, by quickly diffused intelligence, can be rapidly assembled, can cooperate far more readily than those who are scattered through rural districts. With all which direct and indirect results of industrial development must be joined the ultimate result upon character, produced by daily fulfilling and enforcing contracts—a discipline which, while requiring each man to recognize the claims of others, also requires him to maintain his own. In Solon himself this attitude which joins assertion of personal rights with respect for the rights of others was well exemplified; since, when his influence was great he refused to become a despot, though pressed to do so, and in his latter days he resisted at the risk of death the establishment of a despotism. In various ways, then, increasing industrial activity tended to when the original oligarchic form, and initiate a more popular form. And though these effects of industrialism, joined with subsequently-accumulated effects, were for a long time held in check by the usurping Peisistratidæ, yet, being ready to show themselves when, some time after the expulsion of these tyrants, there came the Kleisthenian revolution, they were doubtless instrumental in then initiating the popular form of government.

Though not in so great a degree, yet in some degree, the same causes operated in liberalizing and widening the Roman oligarchy. Rome "was indebted for the commencement of its importance to international commerce"; and, as Mommsen points out, "the distinction between Rome and the mass of the other Latin towns must certainly be traced back to its commercial position, and to the type of character produced by that position. . . . Rome was the emporium of the Latin districts." Moreover, as in Athens, though doubtless to a smaller extent, trade brought an increasing settlement of strangers, to whom rights were given, and who, joined with emancipated slaves and with clients, less bound to their patrons, formed an industrial population, the eventual inclusion of which in the burgess-body caused that widening of the constitution effected by Servius Tullius.

The Italian republics of later days again show us, in numerous cases, this connection between trading activities and a freer form of rule. The Italian towns were industrial centers. "The merchants of Genoa, Pisa, Florence, and Venice supplied Europe with the products of the Mediterranean and of the East; the bankers of Lombardy instructed the world in the mysteries of finance and foreign exchanges; Italian artificers taught the workmen of other countries the highest skill in the manufactures of steel, iron, bronze, silk, glass, porcelain, and jewelry. Italian shops, with their dazzling array of luxuries, excited the admiration and envy of foreigners from less favored lands." Then, on looking into their histories, we find that industrial guilds were the bases of their political organizations; that the upper mercantile classes became the rulers, in some cases excluding the nobles; and that, while external wars and internal feuds tended continually to revive narrower, or more personal, forms of rule, rebellions of the industrial citizens, from time to time occurring, tended to reestablish popular rule.

When we join with these the like general connections that arose in the Netherlands and in the Hanse towns; when we remember the liberalization of our own political institutions which has gone along with growing industrialism; when we observe that the towns more than the country, and the great industrial centers more than the small ones, have given the impulses to these changes—it becomes unquestionable that, while by increase of militant activities compound headships are narrowed, they are widened in proportion as industrial activities become predominant.

In common with the results reached in preceding chapters, the results above reached show that types of political organization are not matters of deliberate choice. It is common to speak of a society as though it had, once upon a time, decided on the form of government which thereafter existed in it. Even Mr. Grote, in his comparison between the institutions of ancient Greece and those of mediæval Europe (vol. iii, pages 10-12) tacitly implies that conceptions of the advantages or disadvantages of this or that arrangement furnished motives for establishing or maintaining it. But, as gathered together in the foregoing sections, the facts show us that, as with the genesis of simple political headships, so with the genesis of compound political headships, conditions and not intentions determine.

Recognizing the fact that independence of character is a factor, but ascribing this independence of character to the continued existence of a race in a habitat which facilitates evasion of control, we saw that, with such a nature so conditioned, cooperation in war causes the union on equal terms of groups whose heads are joined to form a directive council. And according as the component groups are governed more or less autocratically, the directive council is more or less oligarchic. We have seen that in localities differing so widely as do mountain-regions, marshes or mud-islands, and jungles, men of different races have developed political heads of this compound kind. And, on observing that the localities, otherwise so unlike, are alike as being severally made up of parts difficult of access, we cannot question that to this is mainly due the governmental form under which their inhabitants unite.

Besides the compound headships which are thus indigenous in places favoring them, there are other compound headships which arise after the break-up of preceding political organizations. Especially apt are they so to arise where the people, not scattered through a wide district but concentrated in a town, can assemble bodily. Control of every kind having disappeared, it happens in such cases that the aggregate will has free play, and there establishes itself for a time that relatively popular form with which all government begins; but, regularly or irregularly, a superior few become differentiated from the many, and of predominant men someone is made, directly or indirectly, most predominant.

Compound headships habitually become, in course of time, either narrower or wider. They are narrowed by militancy, which tends ever to concentrate directive power in fewer hands, and, if continued, almost certainly changes them into simple headships. Conversely, they are widened by industrialism. This, by gathering together aliens detached from the restraints imposed by patriarchal, feudal, or other such organizations, by increasing the number of those to be coerced in comparison with the number of those who have to coerce them, by placing this larger number in conditions favoring concerted action, by substituting for daily enforced obedience the daily fulfillment of voluntary obligations and daily maintenance of claims, tends ever toward equalization of citizenship.

VIII. Consultative Bodies

Two parts of the primitive triune political structure have, in the last two chapters, been dealt with separately; or, to speak strictly, the first has been considered as independent of the second, and again, the second as independent of the first: incidentally noting its relations to the third. Here we have to treat of the two in combination. Instead of observing how from the chief, little above the rest, there is, under certain conditions, evolved the absolute ruler, entirely subordinating the select few and the many; and instead of observing how, under other conditions, the select few become an oligarchy tolerating no supreme man, and keeping the multitude in subjection, we have now to observe the cases in which there is established a coöperation between the first and the second.

After chieftainship has become settled, the chief continues to have sundry reasons for acting in concert with his head-men. It is needful to conciliate them; it is needful to get their advice and willing assistance; and, in serious matters, it is desirable to divide responsibility with them. Hence the prevalence of a consultative assembly. In Samoa, "the chief of the village and the heads of families formed, and still form, the legislative body of the place." Among the Foolahs, "before undertaking anything important or declaring war, the king [of Rabbah] is obliged to summon a council of Mallams and the principal people." Of the Mandingo states we read that, "in all affairs of importance, the king calls an assembly of the principal men, or elders, by whose counsels he is directed." And such cases might be multiplied indefinitely.

That we may fully understand the essential nature of this institution, and that we may see why, as it evolves, it assumes the distinctive characters it does, we must once more go back to the beginning.

Evidence, coming from many peoples in all times, shows that the consultative body is, at the outset, nothing more than a council of war. It is in the open-air meeting of armed men that the cluster of leaders is first seen performing that deliberative function in respect of military measures which is afterward extended to other measures. Long after its deliberations have become more general in their scope, there survive traces of this origin.

In Rome, where the king was above all things the general, and where the senators, as the heads of clans, were, at the outset, war chiefs, the burgesses were habitually, when called together, addressed as "spear-men": there survived the title which was naturally given to them when they were present as listeners at war-councils. So, during later days in Italy, when the small republics grew up. Describing the assembling of "citizens at the sound of a great bell, to concert together the means of their common defense," Sismondi says, "This meeting of all the men of the state capable of bearing arms was called a Parliament." Concerning the gatherings of the Poles in early times we read: "Such assemblies, before the establishment of a senate, and while the kings were limited in power, were of frequent occurrence, and. . . were attended by all who bore arms"; and at a later stage "the *comitia paludata,* which assembled during an interregnum, consisted of the whole body of nobles, who attended in the open plain, armed and equipped as if for battle." In Hungary, too, up to the beginning of the sixteenth century, "les seigneurs, à cheval et armés de pied en cap comme pour aller en guerre, se réunissaient dans le champ de courses de Rakos, près de Pesth, et là discutaient en plain air les affaires publiques." Again, "the supreme political council is the nation in arms," says Stubbs of the primitive Germans; and though, during the Merovingian period, the popular power declined, yet, "under Chlodovech and his immediate successors, the people assembled in arms had a real participation in the resolutions of the king." Even now the custom of going weapon in hand is maintained where the primitive political form remains. "To the present day," writes M. Laveleye, "the inhabitants of the Outer Rhodes of Appenzell come to the general assembly, one year at Hundwyl

161

and the other at Trogen, each carrying in his hand an old sword or ancient rapier of the middle ages." Mr. Freeman, too, was witness to a like annual gathering in Uri, where the inhabitants assemble in arms to elect their chief magistrate and to deliberate.

It may, indeed, be alleged that in early, unsettled times the carrying of arms by each freeman was needful for personal safety, especially when a place of meeting very far from his home had to be reached. But there is evidence that, though this continued to be a cause for assembling in arms, it was not by itself a sufficient cause. While we read of the ancient Scandinavians that "all freemen capable of bearing arms were admitted" to the national assembly, and that, after his election from "among the descendants of the sacred stock," "the new sovereign was elevated amid the clash of arms and the shouts of the multitude," we also read that "nobody, not even the king or his champions, were allowed to come armed to the assizes."

Even apart from such evidence, there is ample reason to infer that the council of war originated the consultative body, and gave outlines to its structure. Defense against enemies was everywhere the need which originally prompted joint deliberation. For other purposes individual action, or action in small parties, might suffice; but for insuring the general safety combined action of the whole horde or tribe was necessary; and to secure this combined action must have been the first motive for a political gathering. Moreover, certain constitutional traits of early assemblies, among the civilized, point to councils of war as having initiated them. If we ask what must happen when, in a tribe, the predominant few debate military measures in presence of the many, the reply is that, in the absence of a developed political organization, the assent of the many to any decision must be obtained before it can be acted upon; and the like must at first happen when many tribes are united. As Gibbon says of the Diet of the Tartars, formed of chiefs of tribes and their martial trains, "the monarch who reviews the strength, must consult the inclination, of an armed people." Even if, under such conditions, the predominant few could impose their will upon the many, armed like themselves, it would clearly be impolitic to do so, since success in war would be endangered by dissension. Hence would arise the usage of putting to the surrounding mass of armed men the question whether they agreed to the course which the council of chiefs had decided upon. There would grow up a form such as that which had become established for governmental purposes at large among the early Romans, whose king or general asked the assembled burgesses or "spear-men" whether they approved of the proposal made; or like that ascribed by Tacitus to the primitive Germans, who, now with murmurs and now with brandishing of spears, rejected or accepted the suggestions of their leaders. Moreover, there would naturally come just that restricted expression of popular opinion which we are told of. The Roman burgesses were allowed to answer only "Yes" or "No" to any question put to them; and this is exactly the simple answer which the chief and head warriors would require from the rest of the warriors when war or peace had to be determined upon. A kindred restriction existed among the Spartans. In addition to the senate and coordinate kings, there was "an Ekklesia, or public assembly of citizens, convened for the purpose of approving or rejecting propositions submitted to them, with little or no liberty of discussion"—a usage quite explicable if we assume that in the Homeric Agora, from which the Spartan constitution descended, the assembled chiefs had to gain the assent of their surrounding followers before important actions could be undertaken.

Concluding, then, that war originates political deliberation, and that the select body which especially carries on this deliberation first takes shape on occasions when the public safety has to be provided for, we shall be prepared the better to understand the traits which characterize the consultative body in later stages of its development.

Already we have seen that at the outset the militant class was of necessity the land-owning class. In the savage tribe there are no owners of the tract occupied, save the warriors

163

who use it in common for hunting. During pastoral life, good regions for cattle-feeding are jointly held against intruders by force of arms. And, where the agricultural stage has been reached, communal possession, family possession, and individual possession, have from time to time to be defended by the sword. Hence, as was shown, the fact that in early stages the bearing of arms and the holding of land habitually go together.

While, as among hunting-peoples, land continues to be held in common, the contrasts which arise between the few and the many are such only as result from actual or supposed personal superiority of one kind or other. It is true that, as pointed out, differences of wealth, in the shape of chattels, boats, slaves, etc., cause some class-differentiations; and that thus, even before private land-owning begins, quantity of possessions aids in distinguishing the governing from the governed. When the pastoral state is arrived at and the patriarchal type established, such ownership as there is vests in the eldest son of the eldest; or if, as Sir Henry Maine says, he is to be considered trustee for the group, still his trusteeship joins with his military headship in giving him supremacy. At a later stage, when lands come to be occupied by settled families and communities, and land-ownership gains definiteness, this union of traits in each head of a group becomes more marked; and, as was shown when treating of the differentiation of nobles from freemen, several influences conspire to give the eldest son of the eldest superiority in extent of landed possessions, as well as in degree of power. Nor is this fundamental relation changed when a nobility of service replaces a nobility of birth, and when, as presently happens, the adherents of a conquering invader are rewarded by portions of the subjugated territory, granted on condition of continued military service. Throughout, the tendency continues to be for the class of military superiors to be identical with the class of large land-owners.

It follows, then, that, beginning with the general assemblage of armed freemen, all of them holding land individually or in groups, whose council of leaders, deliberating in presence of the rest, are distinguished only as being the most capable warriors, there will, through frequent wars and progressing consolidations, be produced a state in which this council of leaders becomes further distinguished from the rest by the larger possessions, and consequent greater powers, of its members. Becoming more and more contrasted with the general mass of armed freemen, the consultative body will tend gradually to subordinate it, and, eventually separating itself, will become independent.

The growth of this temporary council of war, in which the king, acting as general, summons to give their advice the leaders of his forces, into the permanent consultative body in which the king, in his capacity of ruler, presides over the deliberations of the same men on public affairs at large, is exemplified in various parts of the world. The consultative body is everywhere composed of minor chiefs, or heads of clans, or feudal lords, in whom the military and civil rule of local groups is habitually joined with wide possessions; and the examples frequently exhibit this composition on both a small and a large scale—both locally and generally. A rude and early form of the arrangement is shown in Africa. Among the Caffres "every chief chooses from among his most wealthy subjects five or six, who act as counselors to him. . . . The great council of the king is composed of the chiefs of particular kraals." A Bechuana tribe "generally includes a number of towns or villages, each having its distinct head, under whom there are a number of subordinate chiefs," who "all acknowledge the supremacy of the principal one. His power, though very great and in some instances despotic, is, nevertheless, controlled by the minor chiefs, who, in their *pichos* or *pitshos* their parliament or public meetings, use the greatest plainness of speech in exposing what they consider culpable or lax in his government." Of the Wanyamwezi. Burton says that the Sultan is "surrounded by a council, varying from two to a score of chiefs and elders. . . . His authority is circumscribed by a rude balance of power; the chiefs around him can probably bring as many warriors into the field as he can." Similarly in Ashantee. "The caboceers and captains. . . claim to be heard on all questions relating to war and foreign politics. Such matters are considered in a general assembly, and the king sometimes finds it prudent to yield to the views and urgent representations of the majority." From the ancient American states, too, instances may be cited. In Mexico "general assemblies were presided over by the king every eighty days. They came to these meetings from all parts of the country"; and then we read further that the highest rank of nobility, the Teuctli, "took precedence of all others in the senate, both in the order of sitting and voting," showing what was the composition of the senate. It was so, too, with the Central Americans of Vera Paz: "Though the supreme rule was exercised by a king, there were inferior lords as his coadjutors, who mostly were titled lords and vassals; they formed the royal council, . . . and joined the king in his palace as often as they were called upon." Turning to Europe, mention may first be made of ancient Poland. Originally formed of independent tribes, "each governed by its own *kniaz,* or judge, whom age or reputed wisdom had raised to that dignity," and each led in war by a temporary *voivod* or captain, these tribes had, in the course of that compounding and recompounding which wars produced, differentiated into classes of nobles and serfs, over whom was an elected king. Of the organization which existed before the king lost his power, we are told that—

Though each of these palatines, bishops, and barons, could thus advise his sovereign, the formation of a regular senate was slow, and completed only when experience had proved its utility. At first, the only subjects on which the monarch deliberated with his barons related to war; what he originally granted through courtesy, or through diffidence in himself, or with a view to lessen his responsibility in case of failure, *they* eventually claimed as a right.

So, too, during internal wars and wars against Rome, the primitive Germanic tribes, once semi-nomadic and but slightly organized, passing through the stage in which armed chiefs and freemen periodically assembled for deliberations on war and other matters, evolved a kindred structure. In Charlemagne's time, at the great assembly of the year—

The dukes, counts, bishops, scabini, and centenaries—all who were connected with the government or the administration—were officially present; the great and small proprietors, the barons and gentry, were so in virtue of their fiefs, the freemen in virtue of their character as warriors, though undoubtedly there were few freemen obliged to bear arms not provided with some portion of landed property.

And then at a later period, as Hallam writes—

In all the German principalities a form of limited monarchy prevailed, reflecting, on a reduced scale, the general constitution of the empire. As the emperors shared their legislative sovereignty with the Diet, so all the princes who belonged to that assembly had their own provincial states, composed of their feudal vassals and of their mediate towns within their territory—

the mass of the rural population having thus ceased to possess power. Similarly during the later feudal period in France. An "ordinance of 1228, respecting the heretics of Languedoc, is rendered with the advice of our great men and prudhommes"; and one "of 1246, concerning levies and redemptions in Anjou and Maine," says that, "having called around us, at Orleans, the barons and great men of the said counties, and having held attentive counsel with them," etc.

To meet the probable criticism that no notice has been taken of the ecclesiastics usually included in the consultative body, it is needful to point out that due recognition of them does not involve any essential change in the account above given. Though modern usages lead us to think of the priest-class as distinct from the warrior-class, yet it was not originally distinct. With the truth that, habitually in militant societies, the king is at once commander-in-chief and high-priest, carrying out in both capacities the dictates of his deity, we may join the truth that the subordinate priest is usually a direct or indirect aider of the wars thus supposed to be divinely prompted. In illustration of the one truth may be cited the fact that, before going to war, Radama, King of Madagascar, "acting as priest as well as general, sacrificed a cock and a heifer, and offered a prayer at the tomb of Andria-Masina, his most renowned ancestor." And in illustration of the other truth may be cited the fact that, among the Hebrews, whose priests accompanied the army to battle, we read of Samuel, a priest from childhood upward, as conveying to Saul God's command to "smite Amalek," and as having himself hewed Agag in pieces. More or less active participation in war by priests we everywhere find in savage and semi-civilized societies; as among the Dakotas, Mundrucus, Abipones, Khonds, whose priests decide on the time for war, or give the signal for attack; as among the Tahitians, whose priests "bore arms, and marched with the warriors to battle"; as among the Mexicans, whose priests, the habitual instigators of wars, accompanied their idols in front of the army, and "sacrificed the first-taken prisoners" at once; as among the ancient Egyptians, of whom we read that "the priest of a god was often a military or naval commander." And the naturalness of the connection, thus common in rude and in ancient societies, is shown by its revival in later societies, notwithstanding an adverse creed. After Christianity had passed out of its early extra-political stage into the stage in which it became a state religion, its priests, during actively militant periods, reacquired the primitive militant character. "By the middle of the eighth century [in France], regular military service on the part of the clergy was already fully developed." In the early feudal period, bishops, abbots, and priors, became feudal lords, with all the powers and responsibilities attaching to their positions: they had bodies of troops in their pay, took towns and fortresses, sustained sieges, led or sent troops in aid of kings. And Orderic, in 1094, describes the priests as leading their parishioners to battle, and the abbots their vassals. Though in recent times Church dignitaries do not actively participate in war, yet their advisatory function respecting it—often prompting rather than restraining—has not even now ceased, as among ourselves was lately shown in the vote of the bishops, who, with one exception, approved the invasion of Afghanistan.

That the consultative body habitually includes ecclesiastics, does not, therefore, conflict with the statement that, beginning as a war council, it grows into a permanent assembly of minor military heads.

Under a different form there is here partially repeated what was set forth when treating of oligarchies: the difference arising from inclusion of the king as a cooperative factor. Moreover, much that was before said respecting the influence of war in narrowing oligarchies applies to that narrowing of the primitive consultative assembly by which there is produced from it a body of land-owning military nobles. But that consolidation of small societies into large ones effected by war brings other influences which join in working this result.

In early assemblies of men similarly armed it must happen that though the inferior many will recognize that authority of the superior few which is due to their leaderships as warriors, to their clan-headships, or to their supposed supernatural descent, yet the superior few, conscious that they are no match for the inferior many in a physical contest, will be obliged to treat their opinions with some deference—will not be able completely to monopolize power. But as fast as there progresses that class-differentiation before described, and as fast as the superior few acquire better weapons than the inferior many, or, as among various ancient peoples, have war-chariots, or, as in mediæval Europe, wear coats of mail or plate-armor and are mounted on horses, they, feeling their advantage, will pay less respect to the opinions of the many. And the habit of ignoring their opinions will be followed by the habit of regarding any expression of their opinions as an impertinence.

This gradual usurpation will be furthered by the growth of those bodies of armed dependents with which the superior few surround themselves—mercenaries and others, who, while

169

unconnected with the common freemen, are bound by fealty to their employers. These, too, with better weapons and defensive appliances than the mass, will be led to regard them with contempt, and to aid in subordinating them.

Not only on the occasions of general assemblies, but from day to day in their respective localities, the increasing power of the chiefs thus caused will tend to reduce the freemen more and more to the rank of dependents, and especially so where the military service of such nobles to their king is dispensed with or allowed to lapse, as happened in Denmark about the thirteenth century:

The free peasantry, who were originally independent proprietors of the soil, and had an equal suffrage with the highest nobles in the land, were thus compelled to seek the protection of these powerful lords, and to come under vassalage to some neighboring Herremand or bishop or convent. The provincial diets, or Lands-Ting, were gradually superseded by the general national Parliament of the Dannehof, Adel-Ting, or Herredag; the latter being exclusively composed of the princes, prelates, and other great men of the kingdom. . . . As the influence of the peasantry had declined, while the burghers did not yet enjoy any share of political power, the constitution, although disjointed and fluctuating, was rapidly approaching the form it ultimately assumed—that of a feudal and sacerdotal oligarchy.

A further influence conducing to loss of power by the armed freemen and gain of power by the armed chiefs, who form the consultative body, follows that widening of the occupied area which goes along with the compounding and recompounding of societies. As Richter remarks of the Merovingian period: "Under Chlodovech and his immediate successors, the people assembled in arms had a real participation in the resolutions of the king. But, with the increasing size of the kingdom, the meeting of the entire people became impossible." Only those who lived near the appointed places could attend. Two facts, one already given under another head, may be named as illustrating this effect:

"The greatest national council in Madagascar is an assembly of the people of the capital and the heads of the provinces, districts, towns, villages," etc.; and, speaking of the English Witenagemot, Mr. Freeman says, "Sometimes we find direct mention of the presence of large and popular classes of men, as the citizens of London or Winchester": the implication in both cases being that all freemen had a right to attend, but that only those on the spot could readily avail themselves of the right. This cause for restriction, which is commented upon by Mr. Freeman, operates in several ways. The actual cost of a journey to the place fixed for the meeting, when a kingdom has become large, is too great to be borne by a man who owns but a few acres. Further, there is the indirect cost entailed by loss of time, which, to one who personally labors or superintends labor, is serious. Again, there is the danger, which in turbulent times is considerable, save to those who go with bodies of well-armed retainers. And obviously these deterrent causes must tell where, for the above reasons, the incentives to attend have become small.

Yet another cause cooperates. When the occupied area is large, and therefore the number inhabiting it great, an assembly of all the armed freemen, could they be gathered, would be disabled from taking part in the proceedings, both by its size and by its lack of organization. A multitude made of those who have come from scattered points over a wide country, mostly unknown to one another, unable to hold previous communication, and therefore without plans, as well as without leaders, cannot cope with the relatively small but well-organized body of those having common ideas and acting in concert.

Nor should there be omitted the fact that when the causes above named have conspired to decrease the attendance of men in arms who live far off, and when there grows up the usage of summoning the more important among them, it naturally happens that in course of time the receipt of a summons becomes the authority for attendance, and the absence of a summons becomes equivalent to the absence of a right to attend.

Here, then, are several influences, all directly or indirectly consequent upon war, which join in differentiating the consultative body from the mass of armed freemen out of which it arises.

Given the ruler, and given the consultative body thus arising, there remains to ask. What are the causes of change in their relative powers? Always between these two authorities there must be a struggle—each trying to subordinate the other. Under what conditions, then, is the king enabled to override the consultative body; and under what conditions is the consultative body enabled to override the king?

Inevitably a belief in the superhuman nature of the king gives him an immense advantage in the contest for supremacy. If he is god-descended, open opposition to his will by his advisers is out of the question; and members of his council, singly or in combination, dare do no more than tender humble advice. Moreover, if the line of succession is so settled that there rarely or never occur occasions on which the king has to be elected by the chief men, so that they have no opportunity of choosing one who will conform to their wishes, they are further debarred from maintaining any authority. Hence, habitually; we do not find consultative bodies having an independent *status* in the despotically governed countries of the East, ancient or modern. Though we read of the Egyptian king that "he appears to have been attended in war by the council of the thirty, composed apparently of privy councilors, scribes, and high officers of state," the implication is that the members of this council were functionaries, having such powers only as the king deputed to them. Similarly in Babylonia and Assyria, attendants and others who performed the duties of ministers and advisers to the god-descended rulers did not form established assemblies for deliberative purposes. In ancient Persia, too, there was a like condition. The hereditary king, almost sacred and bearing extravagant titles, though subject to some check from princes and nobles of royal blood who were leaders of the army, and who tendered advice, was not under the restraint of a constituted body of them. Throughout the history of Japan down to our own time a kindred state of things existed. The Daimios were required to be present at the capital during prescribed intervals, as a precaution against insubordination; but they were never, while there, called together to take any share in the government. And hereditary divine kingship, having this as its concomitant in Japan, has it likewise in China. We read that, "although there is nominally no deliberative or advisatory body in the Chinese Government, and nothing really analogous to a congress, parliament, or *tiers-état,* still necessity compels the Emperor to consult and advise with some of his officers." Nor does Europe fail to yield us evidence of like meaning. I do not refer only to the case of Russia, but more especially to the case of France during the time when monarchy had assumed its most absolute form. In the age when divines like Bossuet taught that "the King is accountable to no one, . . . the whole state is in him, and the will of the whole people is contained in his"—in the age when the King (Louis XIY), "imbued with the idea of his omnipotence and divine mission," "was regarded by his subjects with adoration" he "had extinguished and absorbed even the minutest trace, idea, and recollection of all other authority except that which emanated from himself alone." Along with establishment of hereditary succession and acquirement of divine *prestige,* such power of the other estates as existed in early days had disappeared.

Conversely, there are cases showing that where the king has never had, or does not preserve, the *prestige* of supposed descent from a god, and where he continues to be elective, the power of the consultative body is apt to override the royal power, and eventually to suppress it. The first to be named is that of Rome. Originally "the king convoked the senate when he pleased, and laid before it his questions; no senator might declare his opinion unasked; still less might, the senate meet without being summoned." But here, where the king, though regarded as having divine approval, was not held to be of divine descent, and where, though usually nominated by a predecessor, he was sometimes practically elected by the senate and always submitted to the form of popular approval, the consultative body presently became supreme. "The senate had in course of time been converted, from a corporation intended merely to advise the magistrates, into a board commanding the magistrates, and self-governing." Afterward "the right of nominating and canceling senators, originally belonging to the magistrates, was withdrawn from them"; and, finally, "the irremovable character and life-tenure of the members of the ruling order, who obtained seat and vote, was definitely consolidated": the oligarchic constitution became pronounced. The history of Poland yields another example. After unions of simply-governed tribes had produced small states and generated a nobility, and after these small states had been united, there arose a kingship. At first elective, as kingships habitually are, this continued so—never became hereditary. On the occasion of each election out of the royal clan, there was an opportunity of choosing for king one whose character the turbulent nobles thought fittest for their own purposes; and hence it resulted that the power of the kingship decayed. Eventually—

Of the three orders into which the state was divided, the king, though his authority had been anciently despotic, was the least important. His dignity was unaccompanied with power; he was merely the president of the senate, and the chief judge of the republic.

And then there is the instance furnished by Scandinavia, already named in another relation. Danish, Norwegian, and Swedish kings were originally elective; and, though, on sundry occasions, hereditary succession became for a time the usage, there were repeated lapses into the elective form, with the result that predominance was gained by the feudal chieftains and prelates forming the consultative body.

The second element in the triune political structure is thus, like the first, developed by militancy. By this the ruler is eventually separated from all below him; and by this the superior few become integrated into a deliberative body separated from the inferior many.

That the council of war, formed of leading warriors who debate in presence of their followers, is the germ out of which the consultative body arises, is implied by the survival of usages which show that a political gathering is originally a gathering of armed men. In harmony with this implication are such facts as that, after a comparatively settled state has been reached, the power of the assembled people is limited to accepting or rejecting the proposals made, and that the members of the consultative body, summoned by the ruler, who is also the general, give their opinions only when invited by him to do so.

Nor do we lack clews to the process by which the primitive war council grows, consolidates, and separates itself. Within the warrior class, which is also the land-owning class, war produces increasing differences of wealth, as well as increasing differences of *status;* so that, along with the compounding and recompounding of groups which war brings about, the military leaders come to be distinguished as large land-owners and local rulers. Hence, members of the consultative body become contrasted with the freemen at large, not only as leading warriors are contrasted with their followers, but, still more, as men of wealth and authority.

This increasing contrast between the second and third elements of the triune political body ends in separation when, in course of time, war consolidates large territories. Armed freemen scattered over a wide area are deterred from attending the periodic assemblies by cost of travel, by cost of time, by danger, and also by the experience that multitudes of men, unprepared and unorganized, are helpless in presence of an organized few, better armed and mounted, and with bands of retainers. So that, passing through a time during which only the armed freemen living near the place of meeting attend, there comes a time when even these, not being summoned, are considered as having no right to attend; and thus the consultative body becomes completely differentiated.

175

Changes in the relative powers of the ruler and the consultative body are determined by obvious causes. If the king retains or acquires the repute of supernatural origin or authority, and the law of hereditary succession is so settled as to exclude election, those who might else have formed a consultative body having coordinate power become simply appointed advisers. But, if the king has not the *prestige* of supposed sacred origin or commission, and continues to be elective, then the consultative body retains power, and is liable to become an oligarchy.

Of course, it is not alleged that all consultative bodies have arisen in the way described, or are constituted in like manner. Societies, broken up by wars or dissolved by revolutions, may preserve so little of their primitive organizations that there remain no classes of the kinds out of which such consultative bodies as those described arise. Or, as we see in our own colonies, societies may have been formed in ways which have not fostered classes of land-owning militant chiefs, and therefore do not furnish the elements out of which the consultative body, in its primitive shape, is composed. Under conditions of these kinds the assemblies answering to them, so far as may be in position and function, are formed under the influence of tradition or example; and in default of men of the original kind are formed of others—generally, however, of those who, by position, seniority, or previous official experience, are more eminent than those forming popular assemblies. It is only to what may be called the normal consultative body which grows up during that compounding and recompounding of small societies into large ones which war effects that the foregoing description applies; and the senates, or superior chambers, which arise under later and more complex conditions, may be considered as homologous to them in function and composition so far only as the new conditions permit.

IX. Representative Bodies

Amid the varieties and complexities of political organization, it has proved not impossible to discern the ways in which simple political heads and compound political heads are evolved; and how, under certain conditions, the two become united as ruler and consultative body. But, to see how a representative body arises, proves to be more difficult; for both process and product are more variable. Less specific results must content us.

As hitherto, so again, we must go back to the beginning to take up the clew. Out of that earliest stage of the savage horde in which there is no supremacy beyond that of the man whose strength, or courage, or cunning, gives him predominance, the first step is to the practice of election—deliberate choice of a leader in war. About the conducting of elections in rude tribes travelers are silent: probably the methods used are various. But we have accounts of elections as they were made by European peoples during early times. In ancient Scandinavia, the chief of a province, chosen by the assembled people, was thereupon "elevated amid the clash of arms and the shouts of the multitude"; and among the ancient Germans he was carried on a shield. Recalling, as this ceremony does, the chairing of a newly elected member of Parliament up to recent times, and reminding us that originally among ourselves election was by show of hands, we are taught that the choice of a representative was once identical with the choice of a chief. Our House of Commons had its roots in local gatherings like those in which uncivilized tribes select head warriors.

Besides conscious selection, there occurs among rude peoples selection by lot. The Samoans, for instance, by spinning a cocoanut, which on coming to rest points to one of the surrounding persons, thereby single him out. Early historic races supply illustrations; as the Hebrews in the affair of Saul and Jonathan, and as the Homeric Greeks when fixing on a champion to fight with Hector. In both these last cases there was belief in supernatural interference: the lot was supposed to be divinely determined. And probably at the outset, choice by lot for political purposes among the Athenians, and for military purposes among the Romans, as, also, in later times, the use of the lot for choosing deputies in some of the Italian republics, and in Spain (as in Leon during the twelfth century), was influenced by a kindred belief; though doubtless the desire to give equal chances to rich and poor, or else to assign without dispute a mission which was onerous or dangerous, entered into the motive or was even predominant. Here, however, the fact to be noted is, that this mode of choice which plays a part in representation may also be traced back to the usages of primitive peoples.

So, too, we find foreshadowed the process of delegation. Groups of men who open negotiations, or who make their submission, or who send tribute, habitually appoint certain of their number to act on their behalf. The method is, indeed, in such cases necessitated; since a tribe cannot well perform such actions bodily. Whence, too, it appears that the appointing of representatives is, at the first stage, originated by causes like those which reoriginate it at a later stage. For, as the will of the tribe, readily displayed in its assemblies to its own members, cannot be thus displayed to other tribes, but must, in respect of inter-tribal matters, be communicated by deputy, so, in a large nation, the people of each locality, able to govern themselves locally, but unable to join the peoples of remote localities in deliberations which concern them all, have to send one or more persons to express their will. Distance in both cases changes direct utterance of the popular voice into indirect utterance.

Before observing the conditions under which this singling out of individuals in one or other way for appointed duties comes to be used in the formation of a representative body, we must exclude classes of cases not relevant to our present inquiry. Though representation as ordinarily conceived, and as here to be dealt with, is associated with a popular form of government, yet the connection between them is not a necessary one. In some places and times representation has coexisted with entire exclusion of the masses from power. In Poland, both before and after the so-called republican form was assumed, the central Diet, in addition to senators nominated by the king, was composed of nobles elected in provincial assemblies of nobles: the people at large being powerless and mostly serfs. In Hungary, too, up to recent times, the privileged class, which, even after it had been greatly enlarged, reached only "one twentieth of the adult males," alone formed the basis of representation. "A Hungarian county before the reforms of 1848 might be called a *direct* aristocrat! cal republic," all members of the noble class having a right to join the local assembly and vote in appointing a representative noble to the general Diet, but the inferior classes having no share in the government.

Other representative bodies than those of an exclusively aristocratic kind must be named as not falling within the scope of this chapter. As Duruy remarks: "Antiquity was not as ignorant as is supposed of the representative system. . . . Each Roman province had its general assemblies. . . . Thus the Lycians possessed a true legislative body formed by the deputies of their twenty-three towns. . . . This assembly had even executive functions." And Pavia, Gaul, Spain, all the eastern provinces, and Greece, had like assemblies. But, little as is known of them, the inference is tolerably safe that these were but distantly allied in genesis and position to the bodies we now distinguish as representative. Nor are we concerned with governing senates and councils elected by different divisions of a town-population, such as those which were variously formed in the Italian republics—bodies which served simply as agents whose doings were subject to the directly-expressed approval or disapproval of the assembled citizens. Here we must limit ourselves to that kind of representation which arises in communities occupying areas so large that their members are obliged to exercise by deputies such powers as they possess; and, further, we have to deal exclusively with cases in which the assembled deputies do not replace preexisting political agencies, but coöperate with them.

It will be well to set out by observing, more distinctly than we have hitherto done, what part of the primitive political structure it is from which the representative body, as thus conceived, originates.

Broadly, this question is tacitly answered by the contents of the preceding chapters. For, if, on occasions of public deliberation, the primitive horde spontaneously divides into the inferior many and the superior few, among whom someone is most influential; and if, in the course of the compounding and recompounding of groups which war brings about, the recognized war-chief develops into the king, while the superior few become the consultative body formed of minor military leaders—it follows that any third coordinate political power must be either the mass of the inferior itself, or else some agency acting on its behalf. Truism though this may be called, it is needful here to set it down; since, before inquiring under what circumstances the growth of a representative system follows the growth of popular power, we have to recognize the relation between the two.

The undistinguished mass, retaining a latent supremacy in simple societies not yet politically organized, though it is brought under restraint as fast as war establishes submission, and conquests produce class-differentiations, tends, when occasion permits, to reassert itself. The sentiments and beliefs, organized and transmitted, which, during certain stages of social evolution, lead the many to submit to the few, come, under some circumstances, to be traversed by other sentiments and beliefs. Passing references have been in several places made to these. Here we must consider them *seriatim* and more at length.

One factor in the development of the patriarchal group during the pastoral stage was shown to be the fostering of subordination to its head by war; since, continually, there survived the groups in which subordination was greatest. But,

181

if so, the implication is that, conversely, cessation of war tends to diminish subordination. Members of the compound family, originally living together and fighting together, become less strongly bound in proportion as they have less frequently to cooperate for joint defense under their head. Hence, the more peaceful the state the more independent become the multiplying divisions forming the gens, the phratry, and the tribe. With progress of industrial life arises greater freedom of action—especially among the distantly-related members of the group.

So must it be, too, in a feudally-governed assemblage. While standing quarrels with neighbors are ever leading to local battles; while bodies of men-at-arms are kept ready, and vassals are from time to time summoned to fight; while, as a concomitant of military service, acts of homage are insisted upon—there is maintained a regimental subjection running through the group. But, as fast as aggressions and counter-aggressions become less frequent, the carrying of arras becomes less needful; there is less occasion for the periodic expressions of fealty; and there is a proportionate increase of daily actions carried on without direction of a superior, fostering increased individuality of character.

These changes are furthered by the decline of superstitious beliefs concerning the natures of head-men, general and local. As before shown, the ascription of superhuman origin, or supernatural power, to the king, greatly strengthens his hands; and where the chiefs of component groups have a sacredness due to nearness in blood to the semi-divine ancestor worshiped by all, or are members of an invading, god-descended race, their authority over dependents is largely enforced. By implication, then, anything which undermines ancestor worship, and the system of beliefs accompanying it, favors the growth of popular power. Doubtless the spread of Christianity over Europe, by diminishing the prestige of governors, major and minor, prepared the way for greater independence of the governed.

182

These causes have relatively small effects where the people are scattered. In rural districts the authority of political superiors is weakened with comparative slowness. Even after peace has become habitual, and local heads have lost their semi-sacred characters, there cling to them awe-inspiring traditions; they are not of ordinary flesh and blood. Wealth, which, through long ages, distinguishes the nobleman exclusively, gives him both actual power and the power arising from display. Fixed literally or practically, as the several grades of his inferiors are during days when locomotion is difficult, he long remains for them the solitary sample of a great man: others are known only by hearsay; he is known by experience. Inspection is easily maintained by him over dependent and sub-dependent people; and the disrespectful or rebellious, if they cannot be punished overtly, can be deprived of occupation, or otherwise so hindered in their lives that they must submit or migrate. Down to our own day, the behavior of peasants and farmers to the squire is suggestive of the strong restraints which kept rural populations in semi-servile states after primitive controlling influences had died away.

Converse effects may be expected under converse conditions, namely, where large numbers become closely aggregated. Even if such large numbers are formed of groups severally subordinate to heads of clans, or to feudal superiors, sundry influences combine to diminish subordination. When there are present in the same place many superiors to whom respectively their dependents owe obedience, these superiors tend to dwarf one another. The power of no one is so imposing if there are daily seen others who make like displays. Further, when groups of dependents are mingled, supervision cannot be so well maintained by their heads. And this, which hinders the exercise of control, facilitates combination among those to be controlled; conspiracy is made easier and detection of it more difficult. Again, jealous of one another, as these heads of clustered groups are likely in such circumstances to be, they are prompted severally to strengthen themselves, and to this end, competing for popularity, are tempted to relax the restraints over their inferiors and to give protection to inferiors ill-used by other heads. Still more are their powers undermined when the assemblage comes to include many aliens. As before implied, this, above all causes, favors the growth of popular power. In proportion as immigrants, detached from the gentile or feudal divisions they severally belong to, become numerous, they weaken the structures of the divisions among which they live. Such organization as these strangers fall into is certain to be a looser one; and their influence becomes a dissolving agency to the surrounding organizations.

And here we are brought back to the truth which cannot be too much insisted upon, that growth of popular power is in all ways associated with trading activities. For only by trading activities can many people be brought to live in close contact. Physical necessities maintain the wide dispersion of a rural population; while physical necessities impel the gathering together of those who are commercially occupied. Evidence from various countries and times shows that periodic gatherings for religious rites, or other public purposes, furnish opportunities for buying and selling, which are habitually utilized; and this connection between the assembling of many people and the exchanging of commodities, which first shows itself at intervals, becomes a permanent connection where many people become permanently assembled—where a town grows up in the neighborhood of a temple, or around a stronghold, or in a place where local circumstances favor some manufacture.

Industrial development further aids popular emancipation by generating an order of men whose power, derived from their wealth, competes with, and begins in some cases to exceed, the power of those who previously were alone wealthy—the men of rank. While this initiates a conflict which diminishes the influence previously exercised by patriarchal or feudal heads only, it also initiates a milder form of subordination. Rising, as the rich trader habitually does in early times, from the non-privileged class, the relation between him and those under him is one from which there is excluded the idea of personal subjection. In proportion as the industrial activities become predominant, they make familiar a connection between employer and employed, which differs from the relation between master and slave, or lord and vassal, by not including allegiance. Under earlier conditions there does not exist the idea of detached individual life—life which neither receives protection from a clan-head or feudal superior nor is carried on in obedience to him. But in town-populations, made up largely of refugees, who either become small traders or are employed by large ones, the experience of a relatively independent life becomes common, and the conception of it distinct.

And the form of cooperation distinctive of the industrial state which thus arises fosters the feelings and thoughts appropriate to popular power. In daily usage there is a balancing of claims; and the conception of equity is, generation after generation, made clearer. The relations between employer and employed, and between buyer and seller, can be maintained only on condition that the obligations on either side are fulfilled. Where they are not fulfilled the relation lapses, and leaves outstanding those relations in which they are fulfilled. Commercial success and growth have thus, as their inevitable concomitants, the maintenance of the respective claims of those concerned, and a strengthening consciousness of them.

In brief, then, dissolving in various ways the old relation of *status,* and substituting the new relation of contract (to use Sir Henry Maine's antithesis), progressing industrialism brings together masses of people who by their circumstances are enabled, and by their discipline prompted, to modify the political organization which militancy has bequeathed.

It is common to speak of free forms of government as having been initiated by happy accidents. Antagonisms between different powers in the state, or different factions, have caused one or other to bid for popular support, with the result of increasing popular power. The king's jealousy of the aristocracy has induced him to enlist the sympathies of the

185

people—sometimes serfs, but more frequently citizens—and therefore to favor them; or, otherwise, the people have profited by alliance with the aristocracy in resisting royal tyrannies and exactions. Doubtless, the facts admit of being thus presented. With conflict there habitually goes the desire for allies; and throughout mediaeval Europe, while the struggles between monarchs and barons were chronic, the support of the towns was important. Germany, France, Spain, Hungary, furnish illustrations.

But it is an error to regard occurrences of these kinds as causes of popular power. They are to be regarded rather as the conditions under which the causes take effect. These incidental weakenings of preexisting institutions do but furnish opportunities for the action of the pent-up force which is ready to work political changes. Three factors in this force may be distinguished—the relative mass of those composing the industrial communities as distinguished from those embodied in the older forms of organization; the permanent sentiments and ideas produced in them by their mode of life; and the temporary emotions excited by special acts of oppression or by distress. Let us observe the cooperation of these.

Two instances, occurring first in order of time, are furnished by the Athenian democracy. The condition which preceded the Solonian legislation was one of violent dissension among political factions; and there was also "a general mutiny of the poorer population against the rich, resulting from misery combined with oppression." The more extensive diffusion of power, effected by the revolution which Kleisthenes brought about, occurred under kindred circumstances. The relatively-detached population of immigrant traders had so greatly increased between the time of Solon and that of Kleisthenes that the four original tribes forming the population of Attica had to be replaced by ten. And then this augmented mass, largely composed of men not under clan-discipline, and therefore less easily restrained by the ruling classes, forced itself into predominance at a time when the ruling classes were divided. Though it is said that Kleisthenes, "being vanquished in a party contest with his rival, took the people into partnership"—though the change is represented as being one thus personally initiated yet, in the absence of that voluminous popular will which had long been growing, the political reorganization could not have been made, or, if made, could not have been maintained. The remark which Grote quotes from Aristotle, that "seditions are generated by great causes, but out of small incidents," if altered slightly by writing "political changes" instead of "seditions," fully applies. For clearly, once having been enabled to assert itself, this popular power could not be forthwith excluded. Kleisthenes could not under such circumstances have imposed on so large a mass of men arrangements at variance with their wishes. Practically, therefore, it was the growing industrial power which then produced, and thereafter preserved, the democratic organization. Turning to Italy, we first note that the establishment of the small republics, referred to in a preceding chapter as having been simultaneous with the decay of imperial power, may here be again referred to more specifically as having been simultaneous with that conflict of authorities which caused this decay. Says Sismondi, "The war of investitures gave wing to this universal spirit of liberty and patriotism in all the municipalities of Lombardy, of Piedmont, Venetia, Romagna, and Tuscany." In other words, while the struggle between emperor and pope absorbed the strength of both, it became possible for the people to assert themselves. And at a later time Florence furnished an instance similar in nature if somewhat different in form.

At the moment when "Florence expelled the Medici, that republic was bandied between three different parties." Savonarola took advantage of this state of affairs to urge that the people should reserve their power to themselves, and exercise it by a council. His proposition was agreed to, and this "council was declared sovereign, on the 1st of July, 1495."

In the case of Spain, again, popular power increased during the troubles accompanying the minority of Fernando IV; and of the periodic assemblies subsequently formed by deputies from certain towns (which met without authority of the government) we read that—

The desire of the Government to frustrate the aspiring schemes of the Infantes de la Cerda, and their numerous adherents, made the attachment of these assemblies indispensable. The disputes during the minority of Alfonso XI more than ever favored the pretensions of the third estate. Each of the candidates for the regency paid assiduous court to the municipal authorities, in the hope of obtaining the necessary suffrages.

And how all this was consequent on industrial development appears in the facts that many, if not most, of these associated towns had arisen during a preceding age by the recolonization of regions desolated during the prolonged contests of Moors and Christians; and that these *poblaciones,* or communities of colonists, which, scattered over these vast tracts, grew into prosperous towns, had been formed of serfs and artisans to whom various privileges, including those of self government, were given by royal charter. With which several examples must be joined the example familiar to all. For it was during the struggle between king and barons, when the factions were nearly balanced, and when the town-populations had been by trade so far increased that their aid was important, that they came to play a noticeable part, first as allies in war and afterward as sharers in government. It cannot be doubted that, when summoning to the Parliament of 1265 not only knights of the shire but also deputies from cities and boroughs, Simon de Montfort was prompted by the desire to strengthen himself against the royal party supported by the Pope. And whether he sought thus to increase his adherents or to obtain larger pecuniary means, or both, the implication equally is that the urban populations had become a relatively important part of the nation. This interpretation harmonizes with subsequent events. For, though the representation of towns afterward lapsed, yet it shortly revived, and in 1295 became established. As Hume remarks, such an institution could not *'have attained to so vigorous a growth and have flourished in the midst of such tempests and convulsions," unless it had been one "for which the general state of things had already prepared the nation"; the truth here to be added being that this "general state of things" was the augmented mass, and consequently augmented influence, of the free industrial communities.

Confirmation is supplied by cases showing that power, gained by the people during times when the regal and aristocratic powers are diminished by dissension, is lost again if, while the old organization recovers its stability and activity, industrial growth does not make proportionate progress. Spain, or more strictly Castile, yields an example. Such share in government as was acquired by those industrial communities which grew up during the colonization of the waste lands became, in the space of a few reigns, characterized by wars and consolidations, scarcely more than nominal.

It is instructive to note how that primary incentive to cooperation which initiates social union at large continues afterward to initiate special unions within the general union. For, just as external militancy sets up and carries on the organization of the whole, so does internal militancy set up and carry on the organization of the parts, even when those parts, industrial in their activities, are intrinsically non-militant. On looking into their histories we find that the increasing clusters of people who, forming towns, lead lives essentially distinguished by continuous exchange of services under agreement, develop their governmental structures during their chronic antagonisms with the surrounding militant clusters.

We see, first, that these settlements of traders, growing important and obtaining royal charters, were by doing this placed in quasi-militant positions—became in modified ways holders of fiefs from their king, and had the associated responsibilities. Habitually they paid dues of sundry kinds equivalent in general nature to those paid by feudal tenants; and, like them, they were liable to military service. In Spanish chartered towns "this was absolutely due from every inhabitant"; and "every man of a certain property was bound to serve on horseback or pay a fixed sum." In France "in the charters of incorporation which towns received, the number of troops required was usually expressed." And in the chartered royal burghs of Scotland "every burgess was a direct vassal of the crown."

Next observe that industrial towns, usually formed by coalescence of preexisting rural divisions rendered populous because local circumstances favored some form of trade, and presently becoming places of hiding for fugitives, and of security for escaped serfs, began to stand toward the small feudally-governed groups around them in relations like those in which these stood to one another: competing with them for adherents, and often fortifying themselves.

Again, there is the fact that these cities and boroughs, which by royal charter or otherwise had acquired powers of administering their own affairs, habitually formed within themselves combinations for protective purposes. In England, in Spain, in France, in Germany—sometimes with assent of the king, sometimes notwithstanding his reluctance as in England, sometimes in defiance of him, as in ancient Holland—there rose up guilds, which, having their roots in quasi-religious unions among related persons, presently gave origin to frith-guilds and merchant-guilds; and these, defensive in their relations to one another, formed the basis of that municipal organization which carried on the general defense against aggressing nobles.

Then there is the further fact that, in countries where the antagonisms between these industrial communities and the surrounding militant communities were violent and chronic, the industrial communities combined to defend themselves. In Spain, the *poblaciones,* which when they flourished and grew into large towns were invaded and robbed by adjacent feudal lords, formed leagues for mutual protection; and again, at a later date, there arose under like needs, more extensive confederations of cities and towns, which, under severe penalties for non-fulfillment of the obligations, bound themselves to aid one another in resisting aggressions, whether by king or nobles. In Germany, too, we have the perpetual alliance entered into by sixty towns on the Rhine in 1255, when, during the troubles that followed the deposition of the Emperor Frederick II., the tyranny of the nobles had become insupportable. And we have the kindred unions formed under like incentives in Holland. So that, both in small and in large ways, the industrial groups here and there growing up within a nation are, in many cases, forced by local antagonisms partially to assume activities and structures like those which the nation as a whole is forced to assume in its antagonisms with nations around.

Here the implication chiefly concerning us is that, if industrialism is thus checked by a return to militancy, the growth of popular power is arrested. Especially where, as happened in the Italian republics, defensive war passes into offensive war, and there grows up an ambition to conquer other territories and towns, the free form of government proper to industrial life becomes qualified by, if it does not revert to, the coercive form accompanying militant life. Or where, as happened in Spain, the feuds between towns and nobles continue through long periods, the rise of free institutions is arrested; since, under such conditions, these can be neither that commercial prosperity which produces large urban populations, nor cultivation of the associated mental nature. Whence it may be inferred that the growth of popular power accompanying industrial growth in England was largely due to the comparatively small amount of this warfare between the industrial groups and the feudal groups around them. The effects of the trading life were less interfered with, and the local governing centers, urban and rural, were not prevented from uniting to restrain the general center.

And now let us consider more specifically how the governmental influence of the people is acquired. By the histories of organizations of whatever kind, we are shown that the purpose originally subserved by some arrangement is not always the purpose eventually subserved. It is so here. Assent to obligations rather than assertion of rights has ordinarily initiated the increase of popular power. Even the

191

transformation effected by the revolution of Kleisthenes at Athens took the form of a redistribution of tribes and demes for purposes of taxation and military service. In Rome, too, that enlargement of the oligarchy which occurred under Servius Tullius had for its ostensible motive the imposing on plebeians of obligations which up to that time had been borne exclusively by patricians. But we shall best understand this primitive relation between duty and power, in which the duty is original and the power derived, by going back once more to the beginning.

For when we remember that the primitive political assembly is essentially a war-council, formed of leaders who debate in presence of armed followers; and when we remember that in early stages all free adult males, being warriors, are called on to join in defensive or offensive actions—we see that, originally, the attendance of the armed freemen is in pursuance of the military service to which they are bound, and that such power as, when thus assembled, they exercise, is incidental. Later stages yield clear proofs that this is the normal order; for it recurs where, after a political dissolution, political organization begins *de novo*. Instance the Italian cities, in which, as we have seen, the original "parliaments," summoned for defense by the tocsin, included all the men capable of bearing arms: the obligation to fight coming first, and the right to vote coming second. And, naturally, this duty of attendance survives when the primitive assemblage assumes other functions than those of a militant kind; as witness the before-named fact that among the Scandinavians it was "disreputable for freemen not to attend" the annual assembly; and the further facts that in France the obligation to attend the hundred court in the Merovingian period rested upon all full freemen; that in the Carlovingian period, the "non-attendance is punished by fines and amercements"; that in England the lower freemen, as well as others, were "bound to attend the shire-moot and hundred-moot" under penalty of "large fines for neglect of duty"; and that in the thirteenth century in Holland, when the burghers were assembled for public purposes, judicial or other, "any one ringing the town bell except by general consent, and any one not appearing when it tolls, are liable to a fine."

After recognizing this primitive relation between popular duty and popular power, we shall more clearly understand the relation as it reappears when popular power begins to revive along with the growth of industrialism. For here again the fact meets us that the obligation is primary and the power secondary. It is mainly as furnishing aid to the ruler, generally for war purposes, that the deputies from towns begin to share in public affairs. There recurs under a complex form that which at an early stage we see in a simple form. Let us pause for a moment to observe the transition.

As was shown when treating of "Ceremonial Institutions," the revenues of rulers are derived, at first wholly and afterward partially, from presents. Beginning as irregular and voluntary, the making of presents grows periodic and more or less compulsory. The occasions on which assemblies are called together to discuss public affairs (mainly military operations for which supplies are needed) naturally become the occasions on which the expected gifts are offered and received. When by successful wars the militant king consolidates small societies into a large one—when there comes an "increase of royal power in intension as the kingdom increases in extension" (to quote the luminous expression of Professor Stubbs); and when, as a consequence, the quasi-voluntary gifts become more and more compulsory, though still retaining such names as *donum* and *auxilium*—it generally happens that these exactions, passing a bearable limit, lead to resistance: at first passive and in extreme cases active. If by consequent disturbances the royal power is much weakened, the restoration of order, if it takes place, is likely to take place on the understanding that, with such modifications as may be needful, the primitive system of voluntary gifts shall be reestablished. Thus, when in Spain the death of Sancho I was followed by political dissensions, the deputies from thirty-two places, who assembled at Valladolid, decided that demands made by the king beyond the customary dues should be answered by death of the messenger; and the need for gaining the adhesion of the towns during the conflict with a pretender led to an apparent toleration of this attitude. Similarly in the next century, during disputes as to the regency while Alfonso XI was a minor, the Cortes at Burgos demanded that the towns should "contribute nothing beyond what was prescribed in" their charters. Kindred causes wrought kindred results in France; as when, by an insurrectionary league, Louis Hutin was obliged to grant charters to the nobles and burgesses of Picardy and of Normandy, renouncing the right of imposing undue exactions; and as when, on sundry occasions, the States-General was assembled for the purpose of reconciling the nation to imposts levied to carry on wars. Nor must its familiarity cause us to omit the instance furnished by our own history, when, after preliminary steps toward that end at St. Alban's and St. Edmund's, nobles and people at Runnymede effectually restrained the king from various tyrannies, and, among others, from that of imposing taxes without the consent of his subjects.

And now what followed from arrangements which, with modifications due to local conditions, were arrived at in several countries under similar circumstances? Evidently, when the king, hindered from enforcing unauthorized demands, had to obtain supplies by asking his subjects, or the more powerful of them, his motive for summoning them, or their representatives, became primarily that of getting these supplies. The predominance of this motive for calling together national assemblies may be inferred from its predominance, previously shown in connection with local assemblies; as instance a writ of Henry I concerning shire-moots, in which, professing to restore ancient custom, he says: "I will cause those courts to be summoned when I will for my own sovereign necessity, at my pleasure." To vote money is therefore the primary purpose for which chief men and representatives are assembled.

From the ability to prescribe conditions under which money will be voted, grows the ability, and finally the right, to join in legislation. This connection is vaguely typified in early stages of social evolution. Making gifts and getting redress go together from the beginning. As was said 'of Gulab Singh, when treating of presents, "even in a crowd one could catch his eye by holding up a rupee and crying out, 'Maharajah, a petition.' He would pounce down like a hawk on the money, and, having appropriated it, would patiently hear out the petitioner." I have in the same place given further examples of this relation between yielding support to the governing agency and demanding protection from it; and the examples there given may be enforced by such others as that, among ourselves in early days, "the king's court itself, though the supreme judicature of the kingdom, was open to none that brought not presents to the king," and that, as shown by the exchequer rolls, every remedy for a grievance or security against aggression had to be paid for by a bribe; a state of things which, as Hume remarks, was paralleled on the Continent.

Such being the primitive connection between support of the political head and protection by the political head, the interpretation of the actions of parliamentary bodies, when they arise, becomes clear. Just as, in rude assemblies of king, military chiefs, and armed freemen, preserving in large measure the original form, as those in France during the Merovingian period, the presentation of gifts went along with the transaction of public business, judicial as well as military—just as, in our own ancient shire-moot, local government, including the administration of justice, was accompanied by the furnishing of ships and the payment of "a composition for the feorm-fultum, or sustentation of the king"—so when, with successful resistance to excess of royal power, there came assemblies of nobles and representatives summoned by the king, there reappeared on a higher platform these simultaneous demands for money on the one side and for justice on the other. We may assume it as certain that, with an average humanity, the conflicting egoisms of those concerned will be the main factors; and that on each side the aim will be to give as little, and get as much, as circumstances allow.

195

France, Spain, and England yield examples which unite in showing this.

When Charles V of France, in 1357, dismissing the States-General for alleged encroachments on his rights, raised money by further debasing the coinage, and caused a sedition in Paris which endangered his life, there was, three months later, a reconvocation of the states, in which the petitions of the former assembly were acceded to, while a subsidy for war purposes was voted. And, of an assembled States General in 1366, Hallam writes, "The necessity of restoring the coin is strongly represented as the grand condition upon which they consented to tax the people, who had been long defrauded by the base money of Philip the Fair and his successors." Again, in Spain the incorporated towns, made liable by their charters only for certain payments and services, had continually to resist unauthorized demands; while the kings, continually promising not to take more than their legal and customary dues, were continually breaking their promises. In 1328 Alfonso XI "bound himself not to exact from his people, or cause them to pay, any tax, either partial or general, not hitherto established by law, without the previous grant of all the deputies convened to the Cortes." And how little such pledges were regarded is shown by the fact that, in 1393, the Cortes who made a grant to Henry III annexed the condition that—

he should swear before one of the archbishops not to take or demand any money, service, or loan, or anything else of the cities and towns, nor of individuals belonging to them, on any pretense of necessity, until the three estates of the kingdom should first be duly summoned and assembled in Cortes according to ancient usage.

Similarly in England during the time when parliamentary power was being established. While, with national consolidation, the royal authority had been approaching to absoluteness, there had been, by reaction, arising that resistance which, resulting in the Charter, subsequently initiated the prolonged struggle between the king trying to break through its restraints and his subjects trying to maintain and strengthen them. The twelfth article of the Charter having promised that no scutage or aid, save those which were established, should be imposed without consent of the national council, there perpetually recurred, both before and after the expansion of Parliament, endeavors on the king's part to get supplies without redressing grievances, and endeavors on the part of Parliament to make the voting of supplies contingent on fulfillment of promises to redress grievances.

On the issue of this struggle depended the establishment of popular power, as we are shown by comparing the histories of the French and Spanish Parliaments with that of the English Parliament. Quotations above given prove that the Cortes originally established, and for a time maintained, the right to comply with or to refuse the king's requests for money, and to impose their conditions; but they eventually failed to get their conditions fulfilled.

In the struggling condition of Spanish liberty under Charles I, the Crown began to neglect answering the petitions of Cortes, or to use unsatisfactory generalities of expression. This gave rise to many remonstrances. The deputies insisted, in 1523, on having answers before they granted money. They repeated the same contention in 1525, and obtained a general law, inserted in the Recopilacion, enacting that the king should answer all their petitions before he dissolved the assembly. This, however, was disregarded as before.

And thereafter rapidly went on the decay of parliamentary power. Different in form, but the same in nature, was the change which occurred in France. Having at one time, as shown above, made the granting of money conditional on the obtainment of justice, the States-General was induced to surrender its restraining powers. Charles VII

obtained from the states of the royal domains which met in 1439 that they [the tallies] should be declared permanent, and from 1444 he levied them as such—i. e., uninterruptedly and without previous vote. . . . The permanence of the tallies was extended to the provinces annexed to the crown, but these preserved the right of voting them by their provincial states. . . . In the hands of Charles VII and Louis XI the royal impost tended to be freed from all control. . . . Its amount increased more and more.

Whence, as related by Dareste, it resulted that, "when the tallies and *aides*. . . had been made permanent, the convocation of the States-General ceased to be necessary. They were little more than show assemblies." But, in our own case, during the century succeeding the final establishment of Parliament, continued struggles necessitated by royal evasions, trickeries, and falsehoods, brought an increasing power to withhold supplies until petitions had been attended to.

Admitting that this issue was furthered by the conflicts of political factions, which diminished the coercive power of the king, the truth to be emphasized is that the increase of a free industrial population was its fundamental cause. The calling together knights of the shire, representing the class of small land-owners, which preceded on several occasions the calling together deputies from towns, implied the growing importance of this class as one from which money was to be raised; and, when deputies from towns were summoned to the Parliament of 1295, the form of summons shows that the motive was to get pecuniary aid from portions of the population which had become relatively considerable and rich. Already the king had on more than one occasion sent special agents to shires and boroughs to obtain subsidies from them for his wars. Already he had assembled provincial councils formed of representatives from cities, boroughs, and market-towns, that he might get from them votes of money. And, when the great Parliament was called together, the reason set forth in the writs was, that wars with Wales, Scotland, and France, were endangering the realm; the implication being that the necessity for obtaining supplies led to this recognition of the towns as well as the counties.

So, too, was it in Scotland. The first known occasion on which representatives from burghs entered into political action was when there was urgent need for pecuniary help from all sources—namely, "at Cambuskenneth, on the 15th day of July, 1326, when Bruce claimed from his people a revenue to meet the expenses of his glorious war and the necessities of the state, which was granted to the monarch by the earls, barons, burgesses, and free tenants, in full Parliament assembled."

In which cases, while we are again shown that the obligation is original, and the power derived, we are also shown that it is the increasing mass of those who carry on life by voluntary coöperation instead of compulsory coöperation partly the rural class of small freeholders, and still more the urban class of traders—which initiates popular representation.

Still there remains the question. How does the representative body become separate from the consultative body? Retaining the primitive character of councils of war, national assemblies are at first mixed. The different "arms," as the estates were called in Spain, form a single body. Knights of the shire, when first summoned, acting on behalf of numerous smaller tenants of the king, owing military service, sit and vote with the greater tenants. Standing, as towns originally do, very much in the position of fiefs, those who represent them are not unallied, in legal *status,* to feudal chiefs; and, at first assembling with these, in some cases remain united with them, as appears to have been habitually the case in France and Spain. Under what circumstances, then, do the consultative and representative bodies differentiate? The question is one to which there seems to be no very satisfactory answer.

Quite early we may see foreshadowed a tendency to part, determined by unlikeness of functions. In the Carlovingian period in France there were two annual gatherings: a larger, which all the armed freemen had a right to attend; and a smaller, formed of the greater personages and deliberating on more special affairs.

If the weather was fine, all this passed in the open air; if not, in distinct buildings. . . . When the lay and ecclesiastical lords were. . . separated from the multitude, it remained in their option to sit together, or separately, according to the affairs of which they had to treat.

And that unlikeness of functions is the cause of separation we find evidence in other places and times. Describing the armed national assemblies of the Hungarians, originally mixed, Lévy writes: "La dernière reunion de ce genre eut lieu quelque temps avant la bataille de Mohacs; mais bientôt après, la diète se divisa en deux chambres: la table des magnats et la table des députés." In Scotland, again, in 1367-'68, the three estates having met, and wishing, for reasons of economy and convenience, to be excused from their functions as soon as possible, "elected certain persons to hold parliament, who were divided into two bodies, one for the general affairs of the king and kingdom, and another, a smaller division, for acting as judges upon appeals." In the case of England we find that though, in the writs calling together Simon de Montfort's Parliament, no distinction was made between magnates and deputies, yet when, a generation after, Parliament became established, the writs made a distinction, "counsel is deliberately mentioned in the invitation to the magnates, action and consent in the invitation to representatives." Indeed, it is clear that since the earlier-formed body of magnates was habitually summoned for consultative purposes, especially military, while the representatives afterward added were summoned only to grant money, there existed from the outset a cause for separation. Sundry influences conspired to produce it. Difference of language, still to a considerable extent persisting and impeding joint debate, furnished a reason. Then there was the effect of class-feeling, of which we have definite proof. Though in the same assembly, the deputies from boroughs "sat apart both from the barons and knights, who disdained to mix with such mean personages"; and probably these deputies themselves, little at ease in presence of imposing superiors, preferred sitting separately. Moreover, it was customary for the several estates to submit to taxes in different proportions; and this tended to entail consultation among the members of each body by themselves. Finally, we read that "after they (the deputies) had given their consent to the taxes required of them, their business being then finished, they separated, even though the Parliament still continued to sit, and to canvass the national business." In which last fact we are clearly shown that, though aided by other causes, unlikeness of duties was the essential cause which at length produced a permanent separation between the representative body and the consultative body.

Thus at first of little account, and growing in power only because the free portion of the community occupied in production and distribution grew in mass and importance, so that its petitions, treated with increasing respect and more frequently yielded to, began to originate legislation, the representative body came to be that part of the governing agency which more and more expresses the sentiments and ideas of industrialism. While the monarch and upper house are the products of that ancient *régime* of compulsory cooperation, the spirit of which they still manifest, though in decreasing degrees, the lower house is the product of that modern *régime* of voluntary cooperation which is replacing it; and in an increasing degree this lower house carries out the wishes of people habituated to a daily life regulated by contract instead of by *status*.

To prevent misconception, it must be remarked before summing up, that an account of representative bodies which have been in modern days all at once created is not here called for. Colonial Legislatures, consciously framed in conformity with traditions brought from the mother-country, illustrate the genesis of senatorial and representative bodies in but a restricted sense; showing, as they do, how the structures of parent societies reproduce themselves in derived societies, so far as materials and circumstances allow; but not showing how these structures were originated. Still less need we notice those cases in which, after revolutions, peoples who have lived under despotisms are led by imitation suddenly to establish representative bodies. Here we are concerned only with the gradual evolution of such bodies.

Originally supreme, though passive, the third element in the triune political structure, subjected more and more as militant activity develops its appropriate organization, begins to reacquire power when war ceases to be chronic. Subordination relaxes as fast as it becomes less imperative. Awe of the ruler, local or general, and accompanying manifestations of fealty, decrease; and especially so where the *prestige* of supernatural origin dies out. Where the life is rural, the old relations long survive in qualified forms; but clans or feudal groups clustered together in towns, mingled with numbers of unattached immigrants, become in various ways less controllable; while by their habits their members are educated to increasing independence. The small industrial groups, thus growing up within a nation consolidated and organized by militancy, can but gradually diverge in nature from the rest. For a long time they remain partially militant in their structures and in their relations to other parts of the community. At first chartered towns stand substantially on the footing of fiefs, paying feudal dues and owing military service. They form within themselves unions, more or less coercive in character, for mutual protection. They often carry on wars with adjacent nobles and with one another. They not uncommonly form leagues for joint defense. And, where this semi-militancy of towns is maintained, industrial development and accompanying increase of popular power are arrested.

But, where circumstances have favored manufacturing and commercial activities and growth of the population devoted to them, this, as it becomes a large component of the society, makes its influence felt. The primary obligation to render money and service to the head of the state, often reluctantly complied with, is resisted when the exactions are great; and resistance causes conciliatory measures. There comes asking consent rather than resort to compulsion. If absence of violent local antagonisms permits, then on occasions when the political head, rousing anger by injustice, is also weakened by defections, there comes cooperation with other classes of oppressed subjects. Men originally delegated simply that they may authorize imposed burdens are enabled, as the power behind them increases, more and more firmly to insist on conditions; and the growing practice of yielding to their petitions, as a means to obtaining their aid, initiates the practice of letting them share in legislation.

Finally, in virtue of the general law of organization that difference of functions entails differentiation and division of the parts performing them, there comes a separation. At first summoned to the national assembly for purposes partially like and partially unlike those of its other members, the elected members show a segregating tendency, which, where the industrial portion of the community continues to gain power, ends in the formation of a representative body distinct from the original consultative body.

X. The Militant Type of Society

Preceding chapters have prepared the way for framing conceptions of the two fundamentally-unlike kinds of political organization, proper to the militant life and the industrial life, respectively. It will be instructive here to arrange in coherent order those traits of the militant type already incidentally marked, and to join with them various dependent traits; and in the next chapter to deal in like manner with the traits of the industrial type.

During social evolution there has habitually been a mingling of the two. But we shall find that, alike in theory and in fact, it is possible to trace out with due clearness those opposite characters which distinguish them in their respective complete developments. Especially is the essential nature of the organization which accompanies chronic militancy capable of being inferred *a priori,* and proved *a posteriori* to exist in numerous cases, while the essential nature of the organization accompanying pure industrialism, of which at present we have little experience, will be made clear by opposition, and such illustrations as exist of progress toward it will become recognizable.

In drawing conclusions, two liabilities to error must be guarded against. We have to deal with societies compounded and recompounded in various degrees; and we have to deal with societies which, differing in their stages of culture, have their organizations elaborated to different extents. We shall be misled, therefore, unless our comparisons are such as take account of unlikenesses in size and in civilization. Clearly, characteristics of the militant type which admit of being displayed by a vast nation may not admit of being displayed by a horde of savages, though this is equally militant. Moreover, as institutions take a long time to acquire their finished forms, it is not to be expected that all militant societies will display the structure appropriate to them in its completeness. Rather may we expect that in most cases it will be incompletely displayed.

In face of these difficulties the best course will be to consider, first, what are the several traits which of necessity militancy tends to produce; and then to observe how far these traits are conjointly shown in past and present nations distinguished by militancy. Having contemplated the society ideally organized for war, we shall be prepared to recognize in real societies the character which war has brought about.

For preserving its corporate life, a society is impelled to corporate action; and the preservation of its corporate life is the more probable in proportion as its corporate action is the more complete. For purposes of offense and defense, the forces of individuals have to be combined; and, where every individual contributes his force, the probability of success is greatest. Numbers, natures, and circumstances being equal, it is clear that of two tribes or two larger societies, one of which unites the actions of all its capable members while the other does not, the first will ordinarily be the victor. There must be an habitual survival of communities in which militant cooperation is universal.

This proposition approaches very nearly to a truism. But it is needful here, as a preliminary, clearly to recognize the truth that the social structure evolved by chronic militancy is one in which all men fit for fighting act in concert against other societies. Such further actions as they carry on they can carry on separately; but this action they must carry on jointly.

A society's power of self-preservation will be great in proportion as, besides the direct aid of all who can fight, there is given the indirect aid of all who cannot fight. Supposing them otherwise similar, those communities will survive in which the efforts of combatants are in the greatest degree seconded by those of non-combatants. In a purely militant society, therefore, individuals who do not bear arms have to spend their lives in furthering the maintenance of those who do. Whether, as happens at first, the non-combatants are exclusively the women; or whether, as happens later, the class includes enslaved captives; or whether, as happens later still, it includes serfs, the implication is the same. For, if, of two societies equal in other respects, the first wholly subordinates its workers in this way, while the workers in the second are allowed to retain for themselves the produce of their labor, or more of it than is needful for maintaining them, then, in the second, the warriors, not otherwise supported or supported less fully than they might else be, will have partially to support themselves, and will be so much the less available for war purposes. Hence, in the struggle for existence between such societies, it must usually happen that the first will vanquish the second. The type of society produced by survival of the fittest will be one in which the fighting part includes all who can bear arms and be trusted with arms, while the remaining part serves simply as a parmanent commissariat.

An obvious implication, of a significance to be hereafter pointed out, is that the non-combatant part, occupied in supporting the combatant part, cannot with advantage to the self-preserving power of the society increase beyond the limit at which it efficiently fulfills its purpose. For, otherwise, some who might be fighters are superfluous workers; and the fighting power of the society is made less than it might be. Hence, in the militant type, the tendency is for the body of warriors to bear the largest practicable ratio to the body of workers.

Given two societies of which the members are all either warriors or those who supply the needs of warriors, and, other things equal, supremacy in war will be gained by that in which the efforts of all are most effectually combined. In open warfare joint action triumphs over individual action. Military history is a history of the successes of men trained to move and fight in concert.

Not only must there be in the fighting part a combination such that the powers of its units may be concentrated, but there must be a combination of the subservient part with it. If the two are so separated that they can act independently, the needs of the fighting part will not be adequately met. If to be cut off from a temporary base of operations is dangerous, still more dangerous is it to be cut off from the permanent base of operations—namely, that constituted by the body of non-combatants. This has to be so connected with the body of combatants that its services may be fully available. Evidently, therefore, development of the militant type involves a close binding of the society. As the loose group of savages yields to the solid phalanx, so, other things equal, must the society of which the parts are but feebly held together yield to one in which they are held together by strong bonds.

But, in proportion as men are compelled to cooperate, their self prompted actions are restrained. By as much as the unit becomes merged in the mass, by so much does he lose his individuality as a unit. And this leads us to note the several ways in which evolution of the militant type entails subordination of the citizen.

His life is not his own, but is at the disposal of his society. So long as he remains capable of bearing arms he has no alternative but to fight when called upon; and, where militancy is extreme, he cannot return as a vanquished man under penalty of death.

Of course with this there goes possession of such liberty only as military obligations allow. He is free to pursue his private ends only when the society has no need of him; and, when it has need of him, his actions from hour to hour must conform, not to his own will, but to the public will.

So, too, with his property. Whether, as in many cases, what he holds as private he so holds by permission only, or whether private ownership is recognized, it remains true that in the last resort he is obliged to surrender whatever is demanded for public use.

Briefly, then, under the militant type the individual is owned by the state. While preservation of the society is the primary end, preservation of each member is a secondary end—an end cared for chiefly as subserving the primary end.

207

Fulfillment of these requirements, that there shall be complete corporate action, that to this end the non-combatant part shall be occupied in providing for the combatant part, that the entire aggregate shall be strongly bound together, and that the units composing it must have their individualities in life, liberty, and property, thereby subordinated, presupposes a coercive instrumentality. No such union for corporate action can be achieved without a powerful controlling agency. On remembering the fatal results caused by division of counsels in war, or by separation into factions in face of an enemy, we see that chronic militancy tends to develop a despotism; since, other things equal, those societies will habitually survive in which, by its aid, the corporate action is made more complete.

And this involves a system of centralization. The trait made familiar to us by an army, in which, under a commander-in-chief, there are secondary commanders over large masses, and under these tertiary ones over smaller masses, and so on down to the ultimate divisions, must characterize the social organization at large. A militant society must have a regulative structure of this kind, since otherwise its corporate action can not be made most effectual. Without such grades of governing centers diffused throughout the non-combatant part as well as the combatant part, the entire forces of the aggregate cannot be promptly put forth. Unless the workers are under a control akin to that which the fighters are under, their indirect aid cannot be insured in full amount and with due quickness.

And this is the form of a society characterized by *status*—a society, the members of which stand one toward another in successive grades of subordination. From the despot down to the slave, all are masters of those below and subjects of those above. The relation of the child to the father, of the father to some superior, and so on up to the absolute head, is one in which the individual of lower status is at the mercy of one of higher status.

Otherwise described, the process of militant organization is a process of regimentation, which, primarily taking place in the army, secondarily affects the whole community.

The first indication of this we trace in the fact everywhere visible, that the military head grows into a civil head—mostly at once, and, in exceptional cases, at last, if militancy continues. Beginning as leader in war he becomes ruler in peace; and such regulative policy as he pursues in one sphere, he pursues, so far as conditions permit, in the other. Being, as the non-combatant part is, a permanent commissariat, the principle of graduated subordination is extended to it. Its members come to be directed in a way like that in which the warriors are directed—not literally, since the dispersion of the one and the concentration of the other prevent exact parallelism; but, nevertheless, similarly in principle. Labor is carried on under coercive control; and supervision spreads everywhere.

To suppose that a despotic military head, carrying out daily the inherited traditions of regimental control as the sole form of government known to him, will not impose on the producing classes a kindred control, is to suppose in him sentiments and ideas entirely foreign to his circumstances.

The nature of the militant form of government will be further elucidated on observing that it is both positively regulative and negatively regulative. It does not simply restrain; it also enforces. Besides telling the individual what he shall not do, it tells him what he shall do.

That the government of a fighting body is thus characterized needs no showing. Indeed, commands of the positive kind given to the soldier are more important than those of the negative kind: fighting is done under the one, while order is maintained under the other. But here it chiefly concerns us to note that not only the control of military life, but also the control of civil life, is, under the militant type of government, thus characterized. There are two ways in which the ruling power may deal with the private individual. It may simply limit his actions to those which he can carry on without aggression, direct or indirect, upon others; in which case its action is negatively regulative. Or, besides doing this, it may prescribe the how, and the where, and the when, of his daily actions; may force him to do various things which he would not spontaneously do; may direct in greater or less detail his mode of living; in which case its action is positively regulative. Under the militant type this positively regulative action is widespread and peremptory. The civilian is in a condition as much like that of the soldier as difference of occupation permits.

And this is another way of expressing the truth that the fundamental principle of the militant type is compulsory cooperation. While this is obviously the principle under which the members of the combatant body act, it no less certainly must be the principle acted upon throughout the non-combatant body, if military efficiency is to be great; since, otherwise, the aid which the non-combatant body has to furnish cannot be insured.

That binding together by which the units of a militant society are made into an efficient fighting structure tends to fix the position of each in rank, in occupation, in locality.

In a graduated regulative organization there is resistance to change from a lower to a higher grade. Such change is made difficult by lack of the possessions needed for filling superior positions; and it is made difficult by the opposition of those who already fill them, and can hold inferiors down. Preventing intrusion from below, these transmit their respective places and ranks to their descendants; and, as the principle of inheritance becomes settled, the rigidity of the social structure becomes decided. Only where an "egalitarian despotism" reduces all subjects to the same political status—a condition of decay rather than of development—does the converse state arise.

The principle of inheritance, becoming established in respect of the classes which militancy originates, and fixing the general functions of their members from generation to generation, tends eventually to fix also their special functions. Not only do men of the slave classes and the artisan classes succeed to their respective positions, but they succeed to the particular occupations carried on in them. This, which is a working out of the tendency toward regimentation, is ascribable primarily to the fact that superiors, requiring from each kind of worker his particular product, have an interest in replacing him at death by a capable successor; while he, prompted to get aid in fulfilling of his tasks, has an interest in bringing up a son to his own occupation: the will of the son being powerless against these conspiring interests. Under the system of compulsory cooperation, therefore, the principle of inheritance, spreading through the producing organization, causes a relative rigidity in this also.

And then a kindred effect is shown in the entailed restraints on movement from place to place. In proportion as the individual is subordinated in life, liberty, and property, to his society, it is needful that his whereabout shall be constantly known. Obviously the relation of the soldier to his officer, and of this officer to his superior, is such that each must be ever at hand; and where the militant type is fully developed the like holds throughout the society. The slave cannot leave his appointed abode; the serf is tied to his allotment; the master is not allowed to absent himself from his locality without leave.

So that the corporate action, the combination, the cohesion, the regimentation, which efficient militancy necessitates, imply a structure which strongly resists change.

A further trait of the militant type, naturally accompanying the last, is that organizations other than those forming parts of the state organization are wholly or partially repressed. The public combination occupying all fields, excludes private combinations.

For the achievement of complete corporate action, there must, as we have seen, be a centralized administration, not only throughout the combatant part, but throughout the non-combatant part; and, if there exist unions of citizens which act independently, they in so far diminish the range of this centralized administration. Any structures which are not parts of the state structure serve more or less as limitations to it, and stand in the way of the required unlimited subordination. If private combinations are allowed to exist, it will be on condition of submitting to an official regulation such as greatly restrains independent action; and since private combinations thus officially regulated are inevitably hindered from doing things not conforming to established routine, and are so debarred from improvement, they cannot habitually thrive and grow. Obviously, indeed, such combinations, formed on the principle of voluntary cooperation, are incongruous with the social type formed on the principle of compulsory cooperation. Hence the militant type is characterized by the absence, or comparative rarity, of bodies of citizens associated for commercial purposes, for propagating special religious views, for achieving philanthropic ends, etc.

Private combinations of one kind, however, are congruous with the militant type—the combinations, namely, which are formed for minor defensive or offensive purposes. We have, as examples, those which constitute factions, very general in militant societies; those which assume forms like the primitive guilds, serving for mutual protection; and those which take the shape of secret societies. Of such bodies it may be noted that they fulfill on a small scale ends like those which the whole society fulfills on a large scale—the ends of self-preservation, or aggression, or both. And it may be further noted that these small included societies are organized on the same principle as the large including society—the principle of compulsory cooperation. Their governments are coercive: in some cases even to the extent of killing those of their members who are disobedient.

A remaining fact to be noted is that a society of the militant type tends to evolve a self-sufficient sustaining organization. With its political autonomy there goes what we may call an economic autonomy. Evidently in proportion as it carries on frequent hostilities with surrounding societies, its commercial intercourse with them must be hindered or prevented: exchange of commodities can go on but to a slight extent between those who are continually fighting. A militant society must, therefore, to the greatest degree practicable, provide internally the supplies of all articles needful for carrying on the lives of its members. Such an economic state as that which existed during early feudal times, when, as in France, "the castles made almost all the articles used in them," is a state evidently entailed on groups, small or large, which are in constant antagonism with surrounding groups. If there does not already exist, within any group so circumstanced, an agency for producing some necessary article, inability to obtain it from without will lead to the establishment of an agency for obtaining it within.

Whence it follows that the desire "not to be dependent on foreigners" is one appropriate to the militant type of society. So long as there is danger that the supplies of needful things derived from other countries will be cut off by the breaking out of hostilities, it is imperative that there shall be maintained a power of producing these supplies at home, and that to this end the required structures shall be maintained. Hence there is a manifest direct relation between militant activities and a protectionist policy.

And now having noted the traits which may be expected to establish themselves by survival of the fittest during the struggle for existence among societies, let us observe how these traits are displayed in actual societies, similar in respect of their militancy but otherwise dissimilar.

Of course in small primitive groups, however warlike they may be, we must not look for more than rude outlines of the structure proper to the militant type. Being loosely aggregated, definite arrangement of their parts can be carried but to a small extent. Still, so far as it goes, the evidence is to the point. The fact that habitually the fighting body is coextensive with the adult male population is so familiar that no illustrations are needed. An equally familiar fact is that the women, occupying a servile position, do all the unskilled labor and bear the burdens; with which may be joined the fact that not unfrequently during war they carry the supplies, as in Asia among the Bhils and Khonds, as in Polynesia among the New Caledonians and Sandwich-Islanders, as in America among the

Comanches, Mundrucus, Patagonians: their office as forming the permanent commissariat being thus clearly shown. We see, too, that, where the enslaving of captives has arisen, these also serve to support and aid the combatant class; acting during peace as producers and during war joining the women in attendance on the army, as among the New-Zealanders, or, as among the Malagasy, being then exclusively the carriers of provisions, etc. Again, in these first stages, as in later stages, we are shown that private claims are, in the militant type, overridden by public claims. The life of each man is held subject to the needs of the group; and, by implication, his freedom of action is similarly held. So, too, with his goods; as instance the remark made of the Brazilian Indians, that personal property, recognized but to a limited extent during peace, is scarcely at all recognized during war; and as instance Hearne's statement concerning certain hyperborean tribes of North America when about to make war, that "property of every kind that could be of general use now ceased to be private." To which add the cardinal truth, once more to be repeated, that where no political subordination exists war initiates it. Tacitly or overtly a chief is temporarily acknowledged; and he gains permanent power if war continues. From these beginnings of the militant type which small groups show us, let us pass to its developed forms as shown in larger groups.

"The army, or, what is nearly synonymous, the nation of Dahomey," to quote Burton's words, furnishes us with a good example: the excessive militancy being indicated by the fact that the royal bedroom is paved with skulls of enemies. Here the king is absolute, and is regarded as supernatural in character—he is "the spirit"; and of course he is the religious head—he ordains the priests. He absorbs in himself all powers and all rights: "by the state law of Dahomey. . . all men are slaves to the king." He "is heir to all his subjects"; and he takes from living subjects whatever he likes. When we add that there is a frequent killing of victims to carry messages to the other world, as well as occasions on which numbers are sacrificed to

214

supply deceased kings with attendants, we are shown that life, liberty, and property are at the entire disposal of the state as represented by its head. In both the civil and military organizations the centers and subcenters of control are numerous. Names, very generally given by the king and replacing surnames, change "with every rank of the holder"; and so detailed is the regimentation that "the dignities seem interminable." There are numerous sumptuary laws; and, according to Waitz, no one wears any other clothing or weapons than what the king gives him or allows him. Under penalty of slavery or death "no man must alter the construction of his house, sit upon a chair, or be carried on a hammock, or drink out of a glass," without permission of the king.

The ancient Peruvian empire, gradually established by the conquering Incas, may next be instanced. Here the ruler, divinely descended, sacred, absolute, was the center of a system which minutely controlled all life. His headship was at once military, political, ecclesiastical, judicial; and the entire nation was composed of those who, in the capacity of soldiers, laborers, and officials, were slaves to him and his deified ancestors. Military service was obligatory on all taxable Indians who were capable; and those of them who had served their prescribed terms, formed into reserves, had then to work under state superintendence. The army having heads of ten, fifty, a hundred, five hundred, a thousand, ten thousand, had, besides these, its superior commanders of Inca blood. The community at large was subject to a parallel regimentation: the inhabitants, registered in groups, being under the control of officers over tens, fifties, hundreds, and so on. And through these successive grades of centers reports ascended to the Inca governors of great divisions, passing on from them to the Inca; while his orders descended "from rank to rank till they reached the lowest." There was an ecclesiastical organization, similarly elaborate, having, for example, five classes of diviners; and there was an organization of spies to examine and report upon the doings of the other officers. Everything was under public inspection. There were village officers who overlooked the plowing, sowing, and harvesting. When there was a deficiency of rain, measured quantities of water were supplied by the state. Any who traveled without authority were punished as vagabonds; but, for those who were authorized to travel for public purposes, there were establishments supplying lodging and necessaries. "It was the duty of the decurions to see that the people were clothed"; and the kinds of cloth, decorations, badges, etc., to be worn by the different ranks were all prescribed. Besides this regulation of external life, there was regulation of domestic life. The people were required to "dine and sup with open doors, that the judges might be able to enter freely"; and these judges had to see that the house, clothes, furniture, etc., were kept clean and in order, and the children properly disciplined: those who mismanaged their houses being flogged. Subject to this regulation, the people labored to support this elaborate state organization. The political, religious, and military classes, throughout all their grades, were exempt from tribute, while the laboring classes, when not serving in the army, had to yield up all produce beyond that required for their bare sustenance. Of the whole empire, one third was allotted for supporting the state, one third for supporting the priesthood, who ministered to the manes of ancestors, and the remaining third had to support the workers. Besides giving tribute by tilling the lands of the sun and the king, the workers had to till the lands of the soldiers on duty, as well as those of the incapables. And they had also to pay tribute of clothes, shoes, and arms. Of the lands on which the people maintained themselves, the parts were apportioned to each man according to the size of his family. Similarly with the produce of the flocks. Such moiety of this in each district as was not required for supplying public needs was periodically shorn, and the wool divided by officials. These arrangements were in pursuance of the principle that "the private property of each man was held by favor of the Inca, and according to their laws he had no other title to it." Thus the people, completely possessed by the state in person, property, and labor, transplanted to this or that locality, as the Inca directed, and, when not serving in the army, living under a discipline like that within the army, were units in a centralized regimented machine, moved throughout life to the greatest practicable extent by the Inca's will, and to the least practicable extent by their own wills. And, naturally, along with militant organization thus carried to its ideal limit, there went an almost entire absence of any other organization. They had no money; "they neither sold clothes nor houses nor estates"; and trade was represented among them by scarcely anything more than some bartering of articles of food.

So far as accounts of it go, ancient Egypt presents us with phenomena allied in their general if not in their special characters. Its predominant militancy during its remotest unrecorded times is sufficiently implied by the vast population of slaves who toiled to build the pyramids; and its subsequent continued militancy we are shown alike by the boasting records of its kings, and the delineations of their triumphs on its temple-walls. Along with this form of activity we have, as before, the god-descended ruler, limited in his powers only by the usages transmitted from his divine ancestors, who was at once political head, high-priest, commander-in-chief, and supreme judge. Under him was a centralized organization, of which the civil part was arranged in classes and sub-classes as definite as were those of the militant part. Of the four great social divisions—priests, soldiers, townsmen, or traders, and common people, beneath whom came the slaves— the first contained more than a score of different orders; the second some half-dozen beyond those constituted by military grades; the third nearly a dozen; and the fourth a still greater number. Though within the ruling classes the castes were not so rigorously defined as to prevent change of function in successive generations, yet Herodotus and Diodorus state that industrial occupations descended from father to son; "every particular trade, and manufacture was carried on by its own craftsmen, and none changed from one trade to another." How elaborate was the regimentation may be judged from the detailed account of the staff of officers and workers engaged in one of their vast quarries: the numbers and kinds of functionaries paralleling those of an army. To support this highly-developed regulative organization, civil, military, and sacerdotal—an organization which held exclusive possession of the land—the lower classes labored. "Overseers were set over the wretched people, who were urged to hard work more by the punishment of the stick than words of warning." And whether or not official oversight included domiciliary visits, it at any rate went to the extent of taking note of each family. "Every man was required under pain of death to give an account to the magistrate of how he earned his livelihood."

Take now another ancient society, which, contrasted in sundry respects, shows us, along with habitual militancy, the assumption of structural traits allied in their fundamental characters to those thus far observed. I refer to Sparta. That warfare did not among the Spartans evolve a simple despotic head, while in part due to causes which, as before shown, favor the development of compound political heads, was largely due to the accident of their double kingship: the presence of two divinely-descended chiefs prevented the concentration of power. But though from this cause there continued an imperfectly centralized government, the relation of this government to members of the community was substantially like that of militant governments in general. Notwithstanding the serfdom, and in towns the slavery of the Helots, and notwithstanding the political subordination of the Perioiki, they all, in common with the Spartans proper, were under obligation to military service: the working function of the first, and the trading function, so far as it existed, which was carried on by the second, were subordinate to the militant function with which the third was exclusively occupied. And the civil divisions thus marked reappeared in the military divisions: "At the battle of Platæa every Spartan hoplite had seven Helots, and every Periœki hoplite one Helot to attend him." The extent to which, by the daily military discipline, prescribed military mess, and fixed contributions of food, the individual life of the Spartan was subordinated to the public demands from seven years upward, needs mention only to show the rigidity of the restraints which here, as elsewhere, the militant type imposes—restraints which were further shown in the prescribed age for marriage, the prevention of domestic life, the forbidding of industry or any money-seeking occupation, the interdict of going abroad without leave, and the authorized censorship under which his days and nights were passed. There was fully carried out in Sparta the Greek theory of society, that "the citizen belongs neither to himself nor to his family, but to his city." So that though in this exceptional case chronic militancy was prevented from developing a supreme head, owning the individual citizen in body and estate, yet it developed an essentially identical relation between the community as a whole and its units. The community, exercising its power through a compound head instead of through a simple head, completely enslaved the individual. While the lives and labors of the Helots were devoted exclusively to the support of those who formed the militant organization, the lives and labors of those who formed the militant organization were exclusively devoted to the service of the state—they were slaves with a difference.

Of modern illustrations that furnished by Russia will suffice. Here, again, with the wars which effected conquests and consolidations, came the development of the victorious commander into the absolute ruler, who, if not divine by alleged origin, yet acquired something like divine *prestige.* "All men are equal before God, and the Russian's God is the Emperor," says De Custine; "the supreme governor is so raised above earth that he sees no difference between the serf and the lord." Under the stress of Peter the Great's wars, which, as the nobles complained, took them away from their homes, "not, as formerly, for a single campaign, but for long years," they became "the servants of the state, without privileges, without dignity, subjected to corporal punishment, and burdened with onerous duties from which there was no escape. . . . Any noble who refused to serve ('the state in the army, the fleet, or the civil administration, from boyhood to old age') was not only

219

deprived of his estate, as in the old times, but was declared to be a traitor, and might be condemned to capital punishment." "Under Peter," says Wallace, "all offices, civil and military," were "arranged in fourteen classes or ranks"; and he "defined the obligations of each with microscopic minuteness. After his death the work was carried on in the same spirit, and the tendency reached its climax in the reign of Nicholas." In the words of De Custine, "the tchinn [the name for this organization] is a nation formed into a regiment; it is the military system applied to all classes of society, even to those who never go to war." With this universal regimentation in structure went a regimental discipline. The conduct of life was dictated to the citizens at large in the same way as to soldiers. In the reign of Peter and his successors domestic entertainments were appointed and regulated; the people were compelled to change their costumes; the clergy to cut off their beards; and even the harnessing of horses was according to pattern. Occupations were controlled to the extent that "no boyard could enter any profession, or forsake it when embraced, or retire from public to private life, or dispose of his property, or travel into any foreign country, without the permission of the Czar." This omnipresent rule is well expressed in the close of certain rhymes, for which a military officer was sent to Siberia:

"Tout se fait par ukase ici;
C'est par ukase que l'on voyage,
C'est par ukase que l'on rit."

Taking thus the existing barbarous society of Dahomey, formed of negroes; the extinct semi-civilized empire of the Incas, whose subjects were remote in blood from these; the ancient Egyptian empire peopled by yet other races; the community of the Spartans, again unlike in the type of its men; and the existing Russian nation made up of Slavs and Tartars—we have before us cases in which such similarities of social structure as exist cannot be ascribed to inheritance of a

220

common character by the social units. The immense contrasts between the populations of these several societies, too, varying from millions at the one extreme to thousands at the other, negative the supposition that their common structural traits are consequent on size. Nor can it be supposed that likenesses of conditions in respect of climate, surface, soil, flora, fauna, or likenesses of habits caused by such conditions, can have had anything to do with the likenesses of organization in these societies; for their respective habitats present numerous marked unlikenesses. Such traits as they one and all exhibit, not ascribable to any other cause, must thus be ascribed to the habitual militancy characteristic of them all. The results of induction alone would go far to warrant this ascription; and it is fully warranted by their correspondence with the results of deduction, as set forth above.

Any remaining doubts must disappear on observing how continued militancy is followed by further development of the militant organization. Three illustrations will suffice:

When, during Roman conquests, the tendency for the successful general to become despot, repeatedly displayed, finally took effect—when the title *imperator,* military in its primary meaning, became the title for the civil ruler, showing us on a higher platform that genesis of political headship out of military headship visible from the beginning—when, as usually happens, an increasingly-divine character was acquired by the civil ruler, as shown in the assumption of the severed name Augustus, as well as in the growth of an actual worship of him; there simultaneously became more pronounced those further traits which characterise the militant type in its developed form. Practically, if not nominally, the other powers of the state were absorbed by him. In the words of Duruy, he had—

the right of proposing, that is, of making, laws; of receiving and trying appeals, i. e., the supreme jurisdiction; of arresting by the tribunitian veto every measure and every sentence, i. e., of putting his will in opposition to the laws and magistrates; of summoning the senate or the people, and presiding over it, i.

221

e., of directing the electoral assemblages as he thought tit. And these prerogatives he will have not for a single year, but for life; not in Rome only. . . but throughout the empire; not shared with ten colleagues, but exercised by himself alone; lastly, without any account to render, since he never resigns his office.

Along with these changes went an increase in the number and definiteness of social divisions. The Emperor

placed between himself and the masses a multitude of people regularly classed by categories, and piled one above the other in such a way that this hierarchy, pressing with ail its weight upon the masses underneath, held the people and factious individuals powerless. What remained of the old patrician nobility had the foremost rank in the city; . . . below it came the senatorial nobility, half hereditary; below that the moneyed nobility, or equestrian order—three aristocracies superposed. . . . The sons of senators formed a class intermediate between the senatorial and the equestrian order. . . . In the second century the senatorial families formed an hereditary nobility with privileges.

At the same time the administrative organization was greatly extended and complicated.

Augustus created a large number of new offices, as the superintendence of public works, roads, aqueducts, the Tiber-bed, distribution of corn to the people. . . . He also created numerous offices of procurators for the financial administration of the empire, and in Rome there were one thousand and sixty municipal officers.

The structural character proper to an army spread in a double way: military officers acquired civil functions and functionaries of a civil kind became partially military. The magistrates appointed by the Emperor, tending to replace those appointed by the people, had, along with their civil authority, military authority; and while "under Augustus the prefects of the pretorium were only military chiefs, . . . they gradually possessed themselves of the whole civil authority, and finally became, after the Emperor, the first personages in the empire." Moreover, the governmental structures grew by incorporating bodies of functionaries who were before independent. "In his ardor to organize everything, he aimed at regimenting the law itself, and made an official magistracy of that which had always been a free profession." To enforce the rule of this extended administration, the army was made permanent, and subjected to severe discipline. With the continued growth of the regulating and coercing organization, the drafts on producers increased; and, as was shown by extracts in a previous chapter concerning the Roman *régime* in Egypt and in Gaul, the working part of the community was reduced more and more to the form of a permanent commissariat. In Italy the condition eventually arrived at was one in which vast tracts were "intrusted to freedmen, whose only consideration was how to cultivate the land with the least possible expense, and Low to extract from their laborers the greatest amount of work with the smallest quantity of food."

An example under our immediate observation may next be taken—that of the German Empire. Such traits of the militant type in Germany as were before manifest have, since the late war, become still more manifest. The army, active and passive, including officers and attached functionaries, has been increased by about one hundred thousand men; and changes in 1875 and 1880, making certain reserves more available, have practically caused a further increase of like amount. Moreover, the smaller German states, having in great part surrendered the administration of their several contingents, the German army has become more consolidated; and even the armies of Saxony, Würtemberg, and Bavaria, being subject to imperial supervision, have in so far ceased to be independent. Instead of each year granting military supplies, as had been the practice in Prussia before the formation of the North-German Confederation, the Parliament of the empire was, in 1871, induced to vote the required annual sum for three years thereafter; in 1874 it did the like for the succeeding seven years; and again in 1880 the greatly increased amount for the augmented army was authorized for the seven years following—steps obviously surrendering popular checks on imperial power. Simultaneously, military officialism has been in two ways replacing civil officialism. Subaltern officers are rewarded for long services by appointments to civil posts—local communes being forced to give them the preference to civilians; and not a few members of the higher civil service, and of the universities, as well as teachers in the public schools, having served as "volunteers of one year," become commissioned officers of the Landwehr. During the stuggles of the so-called Kulturkampf, the ecclesiastical organization became more subordinated by the political. Priests suspended by bishops were maintained in their offices; it was made penal for a clergyman publicly to take part against the government; a recalcitrant bishop had his salary stopped; the curriculum for ecclesiastics was prescribed by the state, and examination by state officials required; church discipline was subjected to state approval; and a power of expelling rebellious clergy from the country was established. Passing to the industrial activities we may note—first, that through sundry steps, from 1873 onward, there has been a progressive transfer of railways into the hands of the state; so that, partly by original construction (mainly of lines for military purposes), and partly by purchase, three fourths of all Prussian railways—have been made government property; and the same percentage holds in the other German states: the aim being eventually to make them all imperial. Trade interferences have been extended in various ways by protectionist tariffs, by revival of the usury laws, by restrictions on Sunday labor. Through its postal service the state has assumed industrial functions—presents acceptances, receives money on bills of exchange that are due, as also on ordinary bills, which it gets receipted; and, until stopped by shopkeepers' protests, undertook to procure books from publishers. Lastly there come the measures for extending, directly and indirectly, the control over popular life. On the one hand, there are the laws under which, up to the middle of last year, two hundred and twenty-four socialist societies have been closed, one hundred and eighty periodicals suppressed, three hundred and seventeen books, etc., forbidden, and under which sundry places have been reduced to a partial state of siege. On the other hand, may be named Prince Bismarck's scheme for reestablishing guilds (bodies which by their regulations coerce their members), and his scheme of state insurance, by the help of which the artisan would in a considerable degree have his hands tied. Though these measures have not been carried in the forms proposed, yet the proposal of them sufficiently shows the general tendency. In all which changes we see progress toward a more integrated structure, toward increase of the militant part as compared with* the industrial part, toward the replacing of civil organization by military organization, toward the strengthening of restraints over the individual and regulation of his life in greater detail.

The remaining example to be named is that furnished by our own society since the revival of military activity—a revival which has of late been so marked that our illustrated papers are, week after week, occupied with little else than scenes of warfare. Already in the first volume of "The Principles of Sociology," I have pointed out many ways in which the system of compulsory cooperation characterizing the militant type has been trenching on the system of voluntary cooperation characterizing the industrial type; and, since those passages appeared (July, 1876), other changes in the same direction have taken place. Within the military organization itself, we may note the increasing assimilation of the volunteer forces to the regular army, now going to the extent of a movement for making them available abroad, so that, instead of defensive action for which they were created, they can be used for offensive action; and we may also note that the tendency shown in the army during a past generation to sink the military character whenever possible, by putting on civilian dresses, is now checked by an order to officers in garrison towns to wear their uniforms when off duty, as they do in more militant countries. Whether, since the date named, usurpations of civil functions by military men (which had in 1873-'74 gone to the extent that there were ninety-seven colonels, majors, captains, and lieutenants employed from time to time as inspectors of science and art classes) have gone further I cannot say; but there has been a manifest extension of the military spirit and discipline among the police, with the effect that, wearing helmet-shaped hats, beginning to carry revolvers, and looking on themselves as half soldiers, they have come to speak of the people as "civilians," and in some cases exercise over "civilians" an inspection of a military kind; as instance the chief of the Birmingham police, Major Bond, whose subalterns track home men who are unsteady from drink but quiet, and prosecute them next morning; or as instance the regulation by policemen's commands of the conflicting streams of vehicles in the London streets. To an increasing extent the executive has been overriding the other governmental agencies; as in the Cyprus business, and as in the doings of the Indian Viceroy under secret instructions from home. In various minor ways are shown endeavors to free officialism from popular checks; as in the desire expressed in the House of Lords that the hanging of convicts in prisons, intrusted entirely to the authorities, should have no other witnesses; and as in the advice given by the late Home Secretary (on May 11, 1878) to the Derby town council, that it should not interfere with the chief constable (a military man) in his government of the force under him—a step toward centralizing local police control in the home office. Simultaneously we see various actual or prospective extensions of public agency, replacing or restraining private agency. There is the "endowment of research," which, already partially carried out by a government fund, many wish to carry further; there is the proposed act for establishing a registration of authorized teachers; there is the bill which provides central inspection for local public libraries; there is the scheme for compulsory insurance—a scheme showing us in an instructive manner the way in which the regulating policy extends itself: compulsory charity having generated improvidence, there comes compulsory insurance as a remedy for the improvidence. Other proclivities toward institutions belonging to the militant type are seen in the increasing demand for some form of protection, and in the lamentations uttered by the "society papers" that dueling has gone out. Nay, even through the party which by position and function is antagonistic to militancy, we see that militant discipline is spreading; for the caucus-system, established for the better organization of liberalism, is one which necessarily, in a greater or less degree, centralizes authority and controls individual action.

Besides seeing, then, that the traits to be inferred *a priori* as characterizing the militant type constantly exist in societies which are permanently militant in high degrees, we also see that in other societies increase of militant activity is followed by development of such traits.

In some places I have stated, and in other places implied, that a necessary relation exists between the structure of a society and the natures of its citizens. Here it will be well to observe in detail the characters proper to, and habitually exemplified by, the members of a typically militant society.

Other things equal, a society will be successful in war in proportion as its members are endowed with bodily vigor and courage. And, on the average, among conflicting societies there will be a survival and spread of those in which the physical and mental powers called for in battle are not only most marked but also most honored. Egyptian and Assyrian sculptures and inscriptions show us that prowess was the thing above all others thought most worthy of record. Of the words good, just, etc., as used by the ancient Greeks, Grote remarks that they "signify the man of birth, wealth, influence, and daring, whose arm is strong to destroy or to protect, whatever may be the turn of his moral sentiments; while the opposite epithet, bad, designates the poor, lowly, and weak, from whose dispositions, be they ever so virtuous, society has little to hope or to fear." In the identification of virtue with bravery among the Romans, we have a like implication. During early turbulent times throughout Europe, the knightly character, which was

227

the honorable character, primarily included fearlessness: lacking this, good qualities were of no account; but, with this, sins of many kinds were condoned.

If, among antagonist groups of primitive men, some tolerated more than others the killing of their members—if, while some always retaliated, others did not—those which did not retaliate, continually aggressed on with impunity, would either gradually disappear or have to take refuge in undesirable habitats. Hence there is a survival of the unforgiving. Further, the *lex talionis,* primarily arising between antagonist groups, becomes the law within the group; and chronic feuds between component families and clans everywhere proceed upon the general principle of life for life. Under the militant *régime* revenge becomes a virtue, and failure to revenge a disgrace. Among the Feejeeans, who foster anger in their children, it is not infrequent for a man to commit suicide rather than live under an insult—rather than submit to an unavenged injury; and in other cases the dying Feejeean bequeaths the duty of inflicting vengeance to his children. This sentiment and resulting practices we trace among peoples otherwise wholly alien, who are, or have been, actively militant. In the remote East may be instanced. the Japanese. They are taught that "with the slayer of his father a man may not live under the same heaven; against the slayer of his brother a man must never have to go home to fetch a weapon; with the slayer of his friend a man may not live in the same state." And in the West may be instanced France during feudal days, when the relations of one killed or injured were required by custom to retaliate on any relations of the offender even those living at a distance, and knowing nothing of the matter. Down even to the time of the Abbé Brantôme the spirit was such that that ecclesiastic, bequeathing to his nephews the duty of avenging any unredressed wrongs done to him in his old age, says of himself: "I may boast, and I thank God for it, that I never received an injury without being revenged on the author of it." That, where militancy is active, revenge, private as well as public, becomes a duty, is well shown at the present time among the Montenegrins a people who have been at war with the Turks for centuries. "Dans le Montenegro," says Boné, "on dira d'un homme d'une natrie [clan] ayant tué un individu d'une autre: Cette natrie nous doit une tête, et il faut que cette dette soit acquitté, car qui ne se venge pas ne ce sancitie pas."

Where activity in destroying enemies is chronic, destruction will become a source of pleasure; where success in subduing fellow-men is above all things honored, there will arise delight in the forcible exercise of mastery; and, with pride in spoiling the vanquished, will go disregard for the rights of property at large. As it is incredible that men should be courageous in face of foes and cowardly in face of friends, so it is incredible that the other feelings fostered by perpetual conflicts abroad should not come into play at home. We have just seen that, with the pursuit of vengeance outside the society, there goes the pursuit of vengeance inside the society; and whatever other habits of thought and action constant war necessitates must show their effects in the social life at large. Facts from various places and times prove that in militant societies the claims of life, liberty, and property are little regarded. The Dahomans, warlike to the extent that both sexes are warriors, and by whom slave-hunting invasions are, or were, annually undertaken "to furnish funds for the royal exchequer," show their blood-thirstiness by their annual "customs," at which multitudinous victims are publicly slaughtered for the popular gratification. The Feejeeans, again, highly militant in their activities and type of organization, who display their recklessness of life not only by killing their own people for cannibal feasts, but by destroying immense numbers of their infants and by sacrificing victims on trivial occasions, such as launching a new canoe, so much applaud ferocity that to commit a murder is a glory. Early records of Asiatics and Europeans show us the like relation. What accounts there are of the primitive Mongols, who, when united, massacred Western peoples wholesale, show us a chronic reign of violence, both within and without their tribes; while domestic assassinations, which from the beginning have characterized the militant Turks, continue to characterize them down to our own day! In proof that it was so with the Greek and Latin races, it suffices to instance the slaughter of the two thousand Helots by the Spartans, whose brutality was habitual, and the murder of large numbers of suspected citizens by jealous Roman emperors, who also, like their subjects, manifested their love of bloodshed in their arenas. That where life is little regarded there can be but little regard for liberty, follows necessarily: those who do not hesitate to end another's activities by killing him will still less hesitate to restrain his activities by holding him in bondage. Militant savages, whose captives, when not eaten, are enslaved, habitually show us this absence of regard for fellow-men's freedom, which characterizes the members of militant societies in general. How little, under the militant *régime,* more or less markedly displayed in all early historic societies, there was any sentiment against depriving men of their liberties, is sufficiently shown by the fact that even in the teachings of primitive Christianity there was no express condemnation of slavery. Naturally the like holds with the right of property. Where mastery established by force is honorable, claims to possession by the weaker are likely to be little respected by the stronger. In Feejee it is considered chief-like to seize a subject's goods; and theft is virtuous if undiscovered. In Dahomey the king "squeezes" any one as soon as he acquires property. Among the Spartans "the ingenious and successful pilferer gained applause with his booty." In mediaeval Europe with perpetual robberies of one society by another there went perpetual robberies within each society. Under the Merovingians "the murders and crimes it ["The Ecclesiastical History of the Franks"] relates have almost all for their object the possession of the treasure of the murdered persons"; and under Charlemagne plunder by officials was chronic: the moment his back was turned "the provosts of the king appropriated the funds intended to furnish food and clothing for the artisans."

Where warfare is habitual, and the required qualities most needful and therefore most honored, those whose lives do not display them are treated with contempt, and their occupations regarded as dishonorable. In early stages labor is the business of women and of slaves—conquered men and the descendants of conquered men; and trade of every kind, carried on by subject classes, long continues to be identified with lowness of origin and nature. In Dahomey, "agriculture is despised because slaves are employed in it." "The Japanese nobles and placemen, even of secondary rank, entertain a sovereign contempt for traffic." Of the ancient Egyptians Wilkinson says, "Their prejudices against mechanical employments, as far as regarded the soldier, were equally strong as in the rigid Sparta." "For trade and commerce the (ancient) Persians were wont to express extreme contempt," writes Rawlinson. The progress of class differentiation which accompanied the conquering wars of the Romans, was furthered by establishment of the rule that it was disgraceful to take money for work, and also by the law forbidding senators and senators' sons from engaging in speculation. And how great has been the scorn expressed by the militant classes for the trading classes throughout Europe down to quite recent times, needs no showing.

That there may be willingness to risk life for the benefit of the society, there must be much of the feeling called patriotism. Though the belief that it is glorious to die for one's country cannot be regarded as essential, since mercenaries fight without it, yet it is obvious that such a belief must conduce greatly to success in war; and that entire absence of it must be so unfavorable to offensive and defensive action that failure and subjugation, will, other things equal, be likely to result. Hence the sentiment of patriotism will be established by the survival of societies the members of which are most characterized by it.

With this there needs to be united the instinct of obedience. The possibility of that united action by which, other things equal, war is made successful, depends on the readiness of individuals to subordinate their wills to the will of a commander or ruler. Loyalty is essential. In early stages the manifestation of it is but temporary, as among the Araucanians, who, ordinarily showing themselves "repugnant to all subordination, are then (when war is impending) prompt to obey, and submissive to the will of their military sovereign" appointed for the occasion. And with development of the militant type this sentiment becomes permanent. Thus, Erskine tells us that the Feejeeans are intensely loyal: men buried alive in the foundations of a king's house considered themseves honored by being so sacrificed; and the people of a slave district "said it was their duty to become food and sacrifice for the chiefs." So in Dahomey there is felt for the king "a mixture of love and fear, little short of adoration." In ancient Egypt, again, where "blind obedience was the oil which caused the harmonious working of the machinery" of social life, the monuments on every side show with wearisome iteration the daily acts of subordination—of slaves and others to the dead man, of captives to the king, of the king to the gods. Though, for reasons already pointed out, chronic war did not generate in Sparta a supreme political head, to whom there could be shown implicit obedience, yet the obedience shown to the political agency which grew up was profound: individual wills were in all things subordinate to the public will expressed by the established authorities. In primitive Rome, too, in the absence of a divinely-descended king to whom submission could be shown, there was submission to an appointed king, qualified only by expressions of opinion on special occasions; and the principle of absolute obedience, slightly mitigated in the relations of the community as a whole to its ruling agency, was unmitigated within its component groups. And that throughout European history, alike on small and on large scales, we see the sentiment of loyalty dominant where the militant type of structure is pronounced, is a truth that will be admitted without detailed proof.

From these conspicuous traits of nature let us turn to certain consequent traits which are less conspicuous, and which have results of less manifest kinds. Along with loyalty naturally goes faith—the two being, indeed, scarcely separable.

232

Readiness to obey the commander in war implies belief in his military abilities; and readiness to obey him during peace implies belief that his abilities extend to civil affairs also. Imposing on men's imaginations, each new conquest augments his authority. There come more frequent and more decided evidences of his regulative action over men's lives; and these generate the idea that his power is boundless. Unlimited faith in governmental agency is fostered. Generations brought up under a system which controls all affairs, private and public, tacitly assume that affairs can only thus be controlled. Those who have experience of no other *régime* become unable to imagine any other *régime*. In such societies as that of ancient Peru, for example, where, as we have seen, regimental rule was universal, there were no materials for framing the thought of an industrial life spontaneously carried on and spontaneously regulated.

By implication, there result repression of individual initiative and a consequent lack of private enterprise. In proportion as an army becomes organized it is reduced to a state in which the independent action of its members is forbidden. And, in proportion as regimentation pervades the society at large, each member of it, directed or restrained at every turn, has little or no power of conducting his business otherwise than by established routine. Slaves can do only what they are told by their masters; their masters cannot do anything that is unusual without official permission; and no permission is to be obtained from the local authority until superior authorities through their ascending grades have been consulted. Hence the mental state generated is that of passive acceptance and expectancy. Where the militant type is fully developed, everything must be done by public agencies; not only for the reason that these occupy all spheres, but for the further reason that, did they not occupy them, there would arise no other agencies—the prompting ideas and sentiments having been obliterated.

There must be added a concomitant influence on the intellectual nature which cooperates with the moral influences

233

just named. Personal causation is alone recognized, and the conception of impersonal causation is prevented from developing. The primitive man has no idea of cause in the modern sense. The only agents included in his theory of things are living persons and the ghosts of dead persons. All unusual occurrences, together with those usual ones liable to variation, he ascribes to supernatural beings. And this system of interpretration survives through early stages of civilization; as we see, for example, among the Homeric Greeks, by whom wounds, deaths, and escapes in battle, were ascribed to the enmity or the aid of the gods, and by whom good and bad acts were held to be divinely prompted. Continuance and development of militant forms and activities maintain this way of thinking. In the first place it indirectly hinders the discovery of causal relations. The sciences grow out of the arts—begin as generalizations of truths which practice of the arts makes manifest. In proportion as processes of production multiply in their kinds and increase in their complexities, more numerous uniformities come to be recognized; and the ideas of necessary relation and physical cause arise and develop. Consequently, by discouraging industrial progress, militancy checks the replacing of ideas of personal agency by ideas of impersonal agency. In the second place, it does the like by direct repression of intellectual culture. Naturally a life occupied in acquiring knowledge, like a life occupied in industry, is regarded with contempt by a people devoted to war. The Spartans clearly exemplified this relation in ancient times; and it was again exemplified during feudal ages in Europe, when learning was scorned as proper only for clerks and the children of mean people. And obviously, in proportion as warlike activities are antagonistic to the advance of science, they further retard that emancipation from primitive ideas which ends in recognition of natural uniformities. In the third place, and chiefly, the effect in question is produced by the conspicuous and perpetual experience of personal agency which the militant *régime* yields. In the army, from the commander-in-chief down to the private undergoing drill, every movement is directed by a superior; and, throughout the society, in proportion as its regimentation is elaborate, things are hourly seen to go thus or thus, according to the regulating wills of the ruler and his subordinates. In the interpretation of social affairs, personal causation is consequently alone recognized. History comes to be made up of the doings of remarkable men; and it is tacitly assumed that societies have been formed by them. Wholly foreign to the habit of mind as is the thought of impersonal causation, the course of social evolution is unperceived. The natural genesis of social structures and functions is an utterly alien conception, and appears absurd when alleged. The notion of a self-regulating social process is unintelligible. So that militancy molds the citizen into a form not only morally adapted, but intellectually adapted—a form which cannot think away from the entailed system.

In three ways, then, we are shown the character of the militant type of political organization. Observe the congruities which comparison of results discloses.

Certain conditions, manifest *a priori,* have to be fulfilled by a society fitted for preserving itself in presence of antagonist societies. To be in the highest degree efficient, the corporate action needed for preserving the corporate life must be joined in by everyone. Other things equal, the fighting power will be greatest where those who cannot fight labor exclusively to support and help those who can: an evident implication being that the working part shall be no larger than is required for these ends. The efforts of all being utilized directly or indirectly for war, will be most effectual when they are most combined; and, besides union among the combatants, there must be such union of the non-combatants with them as renders the aid of these fully and promptly available. To satisfy these requirements, the life, the actions, and the possessions of each individual must be held at the service of the society. This universal service, this combination, and this merging of individual claims, presuppose a despotic controlling agency. That the will of the soldier-chief may be operative when the aggregate is large, there must be sub-centers and sub sub-centers in descending grades, through whom orders may be conveyed and enforced, both throughout the combatant part and the noncombatant part. As the commander tells the soldier both what he shall not do and what he shall do, so, throughout the militant community at large, the rule is both negatively regulative and positively regulative: it not only restrains, but it directs: the citizen as well as the soldier lives under a system of compulsory cooperation. Development of the militant type involves increasing rigidity, since the cohesion, the combination, the subordination, and the regulation, to which the units of a society are subjected by it, inevitably decrease their ability to change their social positions, their occupations, their localities.

On inspecting sundry societies, past and present, large and small, which are, or have been, characterized in high degrees by militancy, we are shown, *a posteriori,* that amid the differences due to race, to circumstances, and to degrees of development, there are fundamental similarities of the kinds above inferred *a priori.* Modern Dahomey and Russia, as well as ancient Peru, Egypt, and Sparta, exemplify that owning of the individual by the state in life, liberty, and goods, which is proper to a social system adapted for war. And, that, with changes further fitting a society for warlike activities, there spread throughout it an officialism, a dictation, and a superintendence, akin to those under which the soldiery lives, we are shown by imperial Rome, by imperial Germany, and by England since its late aggressive activities.

Lastly comes the evidence furnished by the adapted characters of the men who compose militant societies. Making success in war the highest glory, they are led to identify goodness with bravery and strength. Revenge becomes a sacred duty with them; and, acting at home on the law of retaliation which they act on abroad, they similarly at home as abroad are ready to sacrifice others to self: their sympathies, continually deadened in war, cannot be active during peace. They must have a patriotism which regards the triumph of their society as the supreme end of the action; they must possess the loyalty whence flows obedience to authority; and that they may be obedient they must have abundant faith. With faith in authority and consequent readiness to be directed, naturally goes relatively little power of initiation. The habit of seeing everything officially controlled fosters the belief that official control is everywhere needful; and a course of life which makes personal causation familiar and negatives experience of impersonal causation produces an inability to conceive of any social processes as carried on under self-regulating arrangements. And these traits of individual nature, needful concomitants as we see of the militant type, are those which we observe in the members of actual militant societies.